AUGSBURG – CITYSCAPES

Many greetings from
our town in Germany.

Marina &
Charly

PUBLISHERS: HARALD HOLLO AND WALTER LASS

AUGSBURG
CITYSCAPES

PHOTOGRAPHY: REINHARD EISELE

With contributions by

Angela Bachmair, Lothar Bakker, Götz Beck, Rainer Bonhorst,

Thomas Elsen, Christoph Emmendörffer, Hans Frei,

Judith Gardner, Franz Häußler, Ulrich Heiß, Jürgen Hillesheim, Andrea Kümpfbeck,

Eva Leipprand, Manuela Mayr, Christof Metzger,

Christof Paulus, Bernd Roeck, Sepp Strubel, Christof Trepesch, Ralf Witzler

SATZ UND GRAFIK PARTNER

Dear Readers,

The beauty of Augsburg has been renowned since time immemorial – its mediaeval character, the splendour of the Renaissance, the spaciousness of Maximilianstraße – the "finest street in Germany".

Colourful, varied, multifaceted, this book presents the 2000-year-old city, and its many beauties – those already familiar and those that the tourist (and often even the native) passes by without heed. Readers who would like to get to know the attractions of Augsburg while also catching a glimpse behind the stately façades, who would like to know more and see more, are invited to discover a beautiful city.

The journey of discovery is made easy by clearly structured and richly illustrated chapters: Whether the Cathedral or Lech districts, Maximilianstraße or the Puppenkiste – the content is clearly structured and accessible. For orientation, some chapters are accompanied by detail maps with illustrations and brief descriptions of the main points of interest. An overall street plan is enclosed separately.

The essays by our authors (all of whom are insiders and authorities in their field) provide more than just a description of the main attractions. All, whether born in the area or newcomers, have a special relationship with this city and its rich history and culture, its people and its quality of life. This book thus provides more than just tourist information, more than just well-informed city histories or reflections on art and culture. Seen as a whole, these articles give a sense of something that is otherwise difficult to capture, the special "Augsburg feeling". Defiant nostalgia blends with historically aware responsibility, civic values lying somewhere between the phlegmatic and a tradition of political freedom are reconciled with an outward-looking urbanity, inborn Swabian shrewdness connects with a tolerance that has also been handed down through generations. All that together results in the "urban intimacy" that the poet Thomas Mann valued so much in Augsburg.

This "Augsburg feeling" has permeated this book and the long process of its creation, the discussions with authors and employees, whom the publishers would like to thank warmly at the end of the journey.

In "Augsburg – Cityscapes", fellow citizens will have the special delight of recognising their home town as an urbane feeling, and of seeing the beauties of Augsburg from unfamiliar points of view. We wish visitors looking for something more than just tourist information the pleasures of newly discovering a beautiful city and its mysteries.

Harald Hollo and Walter Laß

ISBN 978-3-935438-08-7

The city of Augsburg developed at the confluence of the Lech (right) and Wertach (left). A view of the union of the two rivers, with the Wolfzahnau meadow wood. Between them, the Wertach canal with its power station.

NATURAL SPACE AND CULTURAL LANDSCAPE

"As the ecologist studying the habits of the snail cannot ignore its shell, so we cannot understand human society and its social development without relating it to the landscape."

The growth of the city of Augsburg and its turbulent history are excellent subject matter for this approach to geography. Nature and landscape formed the starting points of the settlement, and the context for its geographical development. Over the centuries, the extent of the settlement, the type of agrarian exploitation, building methods, trade, economic life and transport, indeed the entire development of the city and its environs, were heavily determined by natural circumstances, such as relief and subterranean geology, climate and water courses, soil and vegetation. Not only the usefulness and suitability of natural resources played a major role, but also people's ambitions and goals in the context of changing political regimes and economic activity in the natural sphere.

However, the geographical history of Augsburg was not determined solely by the conditions of the natural sphere, namely geology, topography and geographical location. Its rise to become a provincial centre of the Roman Empire, an important imperial city and one of the richest municipalities in the

world, and its growth as a metropolis in the 19th/20th centuries were due to human activities and the effects of political forces. The natural sphere was exploited in many different ways, modified in many steps, and developed over the centuries into a habitat, living space and economic sphere, with a striking cultural landscape. The shaping forces of historical processes and architectural structures, in their different aspects, are discussed in the following chapters. This article gives an overview of the natural conditions and interactions with nature and culture that are responsible for the emergence and growth of the city and the shaping of the historical cultural landscape.

Topographical Location and Geology

Augsburg lies amidst the northern alpine foothills, which follow the Alps from Lake Geneva to Vienna and are influenced by these mountains in many ways. The long-distance effect of the Alps finds expression in Augsburg's environs and the geological structure and relief. Topographically, Augsburg lies on a slightly raised spur of land at the junction of the alpine rivers Lech and Wertach. The courses of the two valleys form the join between geologically different landscapes within the Bavarian alpine foothills.

In the east, the wide Lechtal borders with the Tertiary hill country, whose gravel, sand and clay subsoil of the Tertiary period has been formed by numerous rivers and brooks into a hilly zone with sweeping high ridges and gently undulating hilltops. This area was not reached by glacier ice, nor flooded by streams of melt-water and covered by ice-age gravel deposits. In the west of Augsburg, the relief is shaped by ranges of hill, which slope gently from south to north with narrow stream valleys and broad box-like valleys between them. Here, the high planes and valley bottoms are covered by moraines for large stretches, while the Tertiary subsoil emerges on the valley slopes in the form of gravel, sand and clay. The Lech and Wertach valleys extend between the hilly landscapes in the east and west as independent landscape units.

For a better understanding of the landscape development, let us take a look at the geological Quaternary age, which began as an "ice age" about 2.5 million years ago and ended about 15,000 years ago. At the beginning of this age of repeated climatic fluctuations, the entire Alpine foothill area was a fairly flat landmass with many rivers on a land surface that sloped gently northwards. The significant changes in the landscape were the result of climatic change. The humid subtropical climate of the Tertiary age, which provided a habitat for various species of elephant and rhinoceros in our area, was followed by a cooling phase with cold and hot periods repeating in succession. The alpine glaciers, remains of which can still be seen in the highest areas of the Alps, increased during the cold period, and penetrated far into the foothills in the form of ice flows. Our area is characterised by advances of the Lech and Wertach glaciers, which extended northwards to different areas, carrying huge amounts of coarse and fine debris. This material was carried by the water streams from the melting ice masses, which we can think of as kilometre-wide rivers in flood, and was deposited as extended drift fields when the impetus weakened.

As a result of special circumstances, these effects of repeated cold periods can be seen in the Augsburg area in the high altitude, the tiering, and the extensive drift deposits.

The oldest debris of the Biber and Danube ice ages lies on the high ridges to the west and covers the so-called "Staudenplatte" and the "Stauffenberg Terrassentreppe" between Schmutter and Zusam. The younger moraines of the Riss and Wuerm ice ages can be seen in the broad valleys of the Lech and Wertach, between the steep gradients of the Lechrain in the east and the Wertachleite to the west and also form the 8–10 metre-high ridges between them. The latter was formed by the interplay of processes of deposition and the cutting of bends by meltwater streams in the course of the last ice age, when the Lech shifted to the east side of the valley, and with increasing erosive force cut into the subsoil. The Wertach appeared at the western edge of this valley, created during the Riss ice age, and also created a terrace edge.

These are the reasons for the conspicuous 3 to 5 kilometre-wide, 8 to 10 metre-high ridge, the elevated terrace between the Lech and Wertach valleys. At the east, it is connected to a narrow 4–6 metre lower strip of land, the Haunstetter low terrace. North of the confluence of the Lech and Wertach, a further elevated terrace continues to the west, separating the broad Lechtal from the Schmuttertal. In the post-glacial period, the Lech and Wertach, with their greater erosive power, cut deeper into the debris deposits, created small terrace steps. The river regulations in the 19th century deepened the flowing waters in the substrate.

Settlement Conditions and Cultural Landscape Development

The flat spur of land between the Lech and Wertach provided favourable conditions for settlement, agriculture and transport. An import legacy of the Wuerm ice age, the loess clay covering on the high terrace, played an important role in this. It was formed from the dust deposits that blew from the vegetation-free areas in the south and west and built up on the loose steppe vegetation during the last cold period. Because of its fine porous structure and high mineral content, the loess provided a fertile soil. The natural forestation with loose oak and beech stocks, made clearance easier and favoured its transformation into farmland. The frequently flooding valley river meadows were, after clearance of

Augsburg and environs as a bird's eye view by Peter Dorisy, 1574.
The landscape is shown naturalistically. The city lies at the confluence of the Lech (foreground) and Wertach (background); it is easy to distinguish the fields and pastures in the valley meadows from agricultural exploitation on the high terrace. The clouds of smoke come from the brickyards. Gouache painting on canvas (detail).

the jungle of alders, ashes, willows and elms, better suited for fields and pastures. Thus, a variegated cultural landscaping of the Augsburg area developed. The cultivated dry, loess-covered high terrace is indicated by the names "Hochfeld" or "Augsburger Feld" for the parcels of land. On the other hand, grassland prevailed on the valley bottoms of the Lech, Wertach and Singold, after the previously continuous riverside woods had been pushed back to a few islands or strips. Significant remainders are Siebentischwald, which is landscaped as a park at the city limit, and the fairly primal Stadtwald. These woodlands, full of water springs and permeated by streams, have played an important role for centuries in providing the city with water for drinking and industrial use, and are therefore subject to nature conservation laws. One special feature is Wolfzahnau, to the north of the city, at the confluence of the two principal watercourses Lech and Wertach, with its varied wet and dry woodland communities and a richly varied biosphere. This valuable and rare natural potential gives a view of

how the natural landscape of the Lech and Wertach valley may once have looked.

The earliest traces of human presence in this area, as far as we know, were in the Mesolithic age, about 8–10,000 years ago. When after the end of the ice age, hunters in search of wild animals, and gatherers of wild fruit passed through the area. A few archaeological findings to the north and south of Augsburg show that people occasionally strayed onto the high terrace. Far more numerous are the Neolithic remains, when the first farmers cleared the woods and planted small farm settlements at the edge of the loess-covered high terrace between the Lech and Wertach. Stone tools and fragments of pottery from almost all periods of the Neolithic (ca. 5800–2000 BC) indicate settlement along the Augsburg high terrace at the boundary of the fertile loess soil and the moist valley meadows. Through the Bronze Age and Urnfield Age (ca. 2000–800 BC), the settlement and grave findings in the Augsburg area multiply. There is a marked increase in the pattern of findings along the eastern edge of the high terrace between Haunstetten and Königsbrunn and the occurrence of grave mounds along the Wertach valley. This burial custom is responsible for numerous early Iron Age grave sites (Hallstatt culture 800–500 BC) between Kriegshaber, Wellenburg, Bergheim and Bobingen. The unearthed remains of jewellery, weapons, pottery and indications of horses and carts are characteristic of a wealthy aristocracy and increasing stratification of society. Economic life still focused on the agricultural mode of living and working, but knowledge of iron working and the use of iron implements and weapons brought innovations for crafts and trade and influenced the social structure.

Since the 5th century BC, Celtic migrants settled in the foothills of the Alps, and are actually named in records as the "Vindelici". The names of the Augsburg rivers Lech and Wertach are also of a Celtic origin and go back to lika/likos = "the stony one" and virdo = "the fast one", terms that indicate their characters as Alpine rivers. There are only scanty settlement and grave findings of the last centuries before Christ. Traces of settlements in Inningen, Haunstetten and Königsbrunn survive, but there has so far been no evidence of an established Celtic presence on the northern part of the spur of land between the Lech and Wertach. The fact that only few prehistoric settlement remains are known in the area of the Augsburg old city is partly because it has been repeatedly built over since Roman times, with the destruction of archaeological findings. In the Augsburg's environs to the west and east, in the extensive wooded areas, late-Celtic quadrangular enclosures, known as "Viereckschanzen", are preserved as striking landscape features, probably as holy places for cult rituals and sacrifices. In the woods to the west and in the vicinity of Aichach, there are other conspicuous landscape features in the form of "funnel pits", which were created during the mining of iron ore. However, we don't know enough about them to assign them to the Celtic period.

The continuous settlement of the Augsburg area since Neolithic times is clear evidence of its suitability for settlement. The cultural landscape was significantly shaped by the Romans, who, following their Alpine campaign in 15 BC, occupied the area as far as

Augsburg around 200 years ago: The coloured etchings by Johann Michael Frey, 1795 (right) and Franz Thomas Weber, 1821 (left), are outstanding examples of the depiction of the city as an element of the cultural landscape and detailed reproduction of nature.

the Danube, and built a legion camp in the present district of Oberhausen. Not long after the Roman legions had withdrawn in 15 AD, civilian settlement on the flood-resistant tongue of land must have started, which, as Augusta Vindelicum, developed into the centre of administration, industry and culture in the Roman province of Rhaetia. It had a variety of ties to the nearby and more distant surroundings. Relicts from farms, graveyards, commercial operations and roads testify to the importance of the Lech and Wertach valleys as focuses of settlement and trade between the Alps and Danube.

Water Abundance and Industry

Decisive factors in the development of a pronounced settlement landscape were the hydrographic conditions, which in turn depend on the geological situation. The Tertiary base beneath the ice age moraines forms a natural reservoir for the groundwater streams flowing from south to north. They emerge at the edge of the high terrace and at the Tertiary/Quaternary boundary layers, and were collected in bucket wells, canals and pipes for centuries and ducted into the city. As factors in the choice of site for the settlements and in particular for the supply of the city with water for drinking and industry, the spring horizons play a much more important role than the rivers, which were difficult to control. The Lech valley with the 10–15 metre thick debris layers could store large volumes of water, which emerge in numerous springs on the valley base, e.g. in the "Meringer Au". By tapping the Lech and building dams, attempts were made to secure the water supply and use the flowing water as an energy resource for industry (grain mills, stamping hammers and hammer mills). The Wertach and Lech rivers served as transport routes for centuries; the Lech had a considerable importance for supplying Augsburg with construction material and fuel, particularly wood. Raft canals and raft landing places were created to bring the raft cargos as close to the city as possible.

The folklorist Wilhelm Heinrich Riehl, a sharp observer of the country and its people, praised the water abundance in his Augsburg studies (1859): "The enigmatic watercourses of this tableland are a true garden of pleasure for the observer. Within the old city boundary of Augsburg, hardly one hour away upstream, a good dozen small brooks spring

amidst the low-lying Lech area, almost at the same height and in the close vicinity of the river, and they run with a will of their own, parallel to one another and to the main stream, often hardly a gunshot apart, cross one another and become confused, and so form new streams. The situation is similar at the Wertach side, with the Singold and its family of brooks. Such a simultaneous collecting and splitting of watercourses was only possible in the moderate Augsburg city area."

When the text was published, the water turbines had already superseded conventional waterwheels as a technical innovation and, as new energy sources, promoted the settlement of industrial areas. Augsburg owes its rise as an important industrial city to its water abundance. To make optimum use of the hydraulic power, while at the same time protecting the settlements and roads against flooding, it was necessary to make technical interventions in the natural water systems. In 1853, work commenced on straightening the Wertach; in 1870, correction work on the Lech between Kaufering and Augsburg began. Starting from the localised riverbank protection structures, cross-structures in the form of weirs were progressively built to prevent the river bed cutting too deep. The energy potential of the rivers was exploited more intensively by leading water into canals. With the creation of barrages and power stations for electricity generation, the river landscape of the Lech and Wertach has been fundamentally reshaped in recent decades.

Importance of the Geographical Position

The geographical situation in the foothills of the Alps has played an important role in the development of the cultural landscape and the rise of the city of Augsburg since the middle ages. Within the geographical constants, the natural conditions offered the ideal conditions for a road junction. For north-south traffic, the Lech and Wertach tals formed the guidelines for the long-distances roads that started from the Alpine crossings. East-west transport, on the other hand, had to cross numerous rivers and surmount the parallel ranges of hills. Crossing the alpine rivers with the broad gravel beds and branched tributaries caused signifi-

cant difficulties. For crossing the Lech, the valley zone upstream of the confluence of the Wertach was therefore more favourable than downstream of the junction of the two voluminous rivers. This circumstance was responsible for Augsburg's function as a bridgehead, which was further promoted by other geographical features. Between the hilly relief in the east and west and the great moors of the north, (Danube-Ried, Danube-Moos), east-west transport through Augsburg was able to use a practical geographical corridor. This line was followed by the great Roman road between Salzburg and Strasbourg, the mediaeval salt and trading routes, the early modern post road, the royal avenue, and not least the Munich-Stuttgart railway line in the 19th century.

Urban development in the middle ages shows the extent to which Augsburg's trans-

The map (1819) shows the city, the villages round about, the distribution of wood and open fields and the transport network. The Lech and Wertach flow on a wide valley bottom and branch into side arms, accompanied by meadow woods. The relief and soil forms are shown hatched.

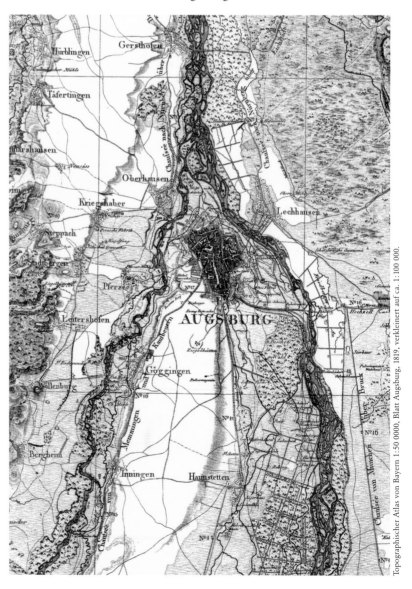

Topographischer Atlas von Bayern 1:50 0000, Blatt Augsburg, 1819, verkleinert auf ca. 1:100 000.

port value was enhanced by the natural-geographical structures and the city's location in the midst of the alpine foothills. When access to southern Europe played a major role in the Italian policy of various emperors and kings, the transport connection to the Alpine crossings had a lasting effect on Augsburg's national importance.

With the expansion of the European long-distance trading network in the 15th and 16th century, Augsburg grew into one of the biggest cities in the empire, and the cityscape was changed forever by energetic building activities. The importance of its transport links subsequently diminished as long-distance trade routes shifted to the Atlantic, territorial states arose, and frontiers were consequently drawn. Augsburg's transports links were eclipsed in the 19th century when Munich took on the function of a railway junction.

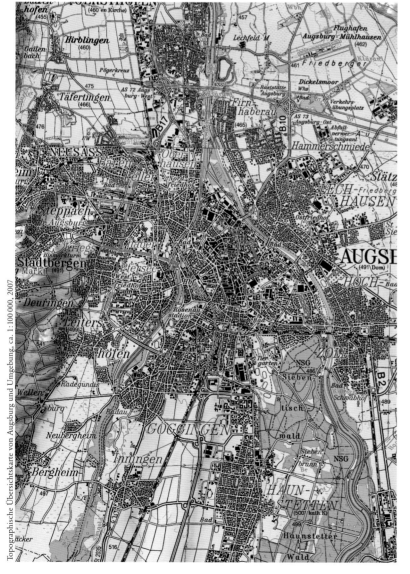

Topographische Übersichtskarte von Augsburg und Umgebung, ca. 1:100 000, 2007

Cultural Landscape and Land Use Today

The natural foundations of the Augsburg settlement and industrial area were predominantly established during the ice age. For almost 8,000 years, people with different needs and using different technologies have exploited the natural area, changed the landscape in many small steps, and left behind their building structures. Over a third of the city area of about 15,000 hectares is now taken up by the demands of living, working, industry, supply and transportation. Another third is claimed by agriculture and gardening. They are mainly distributed over the planes of the Wertach and Lech valley and the loess-covered high terrace.

Natural areas such as woodland, parkland and watercourses still take up almost a third of the city area, amidst an intensive settlement landscape. A major proportion is occupied by the connected riverside woods along the Lech and Wertach, and the extended wooded areas on the western city boundary, within the former Bergheim district. Flowing and standing watercourses take up 2.3 % of the area, forming a rare and exquisite part of the landscape. Together with the green areas and woodlands, they perform an important balancing effect in the natural household, and are an essential leisure and local recreation resource. They also have an effect in profiling the city and shaping the landscape. A major part is played by the biotopes, such as water meadows, strips of wasteland, hedges, copses and near-natural woods. They represent about 8 % of the city area, distributed between around 400 sites. Substantial portions of these are the "city wood" nature conservation area, the "Wertach and Lech meadow" landscape conservation areas including "Wolfzahnau" and protected areas of the landscape such as Wittelsbacher Park and the Kurpark Göggingen. If we compare the topographical maps from 1819 and 2007, we can see the extensive growth and the changed use structure resulting from the profound changes over almost 200 years. The high importance of the natural basis and the near-natural open spaces amidst an intensively utilized cultural landscape emerges quite clearly. Careful husbandry of natural resources will continue to play an important part in future.

Encounters with the Romans

AELIA AVGVSTA

Walking through Augsburg's northern old town, you encounter the Romans literally at every step, but largely without seeing them. For, with a few exceptions, the testaments to the proud capital city of Rhaetia AVGVSTA VINDELICVM = AELIA AVGVSTA, founded under Emperor Augusta, lie buried underground, beneath our feet. For decades, city archaeologists have been continually unearthing wooden and stone remains of the once proud metropolis of the alpine foothills, and numerous everyday findings of its, at the time, ten thousand residents, for admiration in the Roman museum in the former Dominican church of St. Magdalena. This church – built from 1513 to 1515, and surely one of Augsburg's most impressive alongside the Cathedral and Church of St. Ulrich and Afra – has, since 1966, accommodated the archaeological collections from prehistoric to mediaeval times.

Here, in the Roman museum on Dominikanergasse, we first encounter the rich prehistoric findings from Swabia. People have settled here, along the Lech and Danube, ever since they adopted sedentary lifestyles in the seventh millennium before Christ. High-quality findings from settlements, and most of all, graves prove the continuous presence of humans during the entire Neolithic, the Bronze Age (ca. 2000–800 BC) and the subsequent Iron Age until the beginning of Roman domination.

Prominent examples are the drinking service from Ehingen and Unterglauheim with bronze dishes and two gold goblets from the 10th/9th century BC, the wagon burial (ca. 778 BC) from Wehringen, but also the "bell beaker" culture (ca. 2500–2000 BC), the early and late Bronze age and the Urnfield culture (1250–800 BC). During construction of the Land Bureau for Environmental Protection in 1999, remains of a late-Celtic settlement of the last century before the Romans were unearthed for the first time on Augsburg soil! Whom did the "Romans" encounter, when Drusus and Tiberius, the two stepsons of

Augustus, with their troops brought the northern alpine region and the land as far as the Danube under the yoke of Imperium Romanum in 15 BC? Here, the Rhaetians settled in the mountain area, and what is now Switzerland and the alpine foothills was settled by the Vindelici, a subgroup of the Celtic Helvetians. They also included the Licati on the Licca (= Lech). A few years after the conquest, around 8/5 BC, the Romans established what was probably the biggest military camp in the newly subjugated area, at the confluence of the Lech and Wertach: several thousand metal items, their armour, weapons, tools and equipment, were unearthed in Oberhausen in 1910/13 from the gravel of a catastrophic flood in the 1st century BC. Following this natural destruction, the Romans built a new castellum in the 2nd century AD at the east side of the elevated terrace, now free of flooding, from north east of the Cathedral of St. Gallus in the north, to the level of the Mittleres Pfaffengässchen in the south.

The 2,500 to 3,000 occupying force consisted mainly of horsemen, we now know from the findings of recent years but also their

Grave finding of precious bronze tableware and two gold goblets of the Urnfield culture, ca. 1000 BC; discovered in 1834 in Unterglauheim (Dillingen rural district)

The Augsburg treasure trove of 52 gold coins (aurei), after 163/164 AD, hidden during the Markomann wars; discovered in 1978 at St. Stephan.

Relief block of a pillar tomb with picture of a soldier and his wife. Jura limestone, height 1.30 m; found at the Fronhof, 1925 (below).

Pillar tomb for the family of T. Flavius Clemens, soldier in the Legio III Italica. Ca. 200 AD, Jura limestone, height 4.60 m; Augsburg-Oberhausen, 1709 (right).

gravestones. Around the castellum, a civil settlement developments inhabited by the families of the soldiers, traders and workmen. The military camp and surrounding village were burnt down in the civil war unrest of 69/70 AD, after the death of Nero.

In the 1st century AD, the important military centre of AVGVSTA VINDELICVM formed a meeting place – the VIA CLAVDIA AVGVSTA, completed by Emperor Claudius in 46/47 AD, led here. This was the great road leading from upper Italy to the Danube, via the Reschenpass and Fernpass, and subsequently also via the Brenner. A gilded Genius Populi Romani, protector of the Roman state and people, may come from a monument to Emperor Claudius. The settlement at the confluence of the Lech and Wertach, now without an army, was rapidly rebuilt in the last decades of the 1st century AD and enlarged to the west and north. The former castellum area was developed – larger wood buildings for private use and the first public stone buildings were built here. Around 100 AD, the settlement burnt down yet again, as is shown by recent excavation at the Äußeres

Pfaffengässchen. But this destruction (possibly by arson) had an important significance: Now, under Emperor Trajan (98–117), AVGVSTA VINDELICVM had the status of a capital city of the central alpine province of RHAETIA, which ensured it a central role in the area between "Limes" and Upper Italy, between Lake Constance and the river Inn, until well into the 5th century AD, comparable to Munich's role in Bavaria. The governor resided here, the representative of the emperor in Rome, first a knight as procurator, but later, from about 175/180, a senator as legate. He had sweeping powers: principal adjudicator, head of the civil administration and of finances and commander of the troops at the frontier with Rhaetian Limes. The growth in economic and political status of the Roman settlement on the Lech followed as a matter of course – Cambodunum/Kempten had previously performed the function of the governor's residence in the 1st century AD. During the "Markomann wars" around 170/180, Augsburg received a robust city wall with gates – It was certainly built with the help of the Legio III Italica dispatched shortly beforehand to Rhaetia, as we have discovered from the 2003/2004 excavations of its briefly occupied camp in Annahof.

A particularly eminent encounter in the Augsburg of the time is recorded in 121 AD. "AVE! Imperator venit" – "Hurray, the Emperor comes" may have been the cry of the residents when Imperator and Emperor Aelius Hadrianus (117–138) visited Rhaetia on his tour through the provinces. He gave the settlement the official town charter of MVNICIPIVM AELIVM AVGVSTVM. The magistrate of around a hundred councillors was headed by two mayors of equal importance. While the families of city councillors formed the elite class of the civic population (15 city councillors are so far known from inscriptions), a "second class" was formed by new citizens – the "nouveaux riches" and newcomers represented as priests in the "sevir augustalis" for events and the emperor cult. Great importance was placed on the dress regulations: "Clothes make the man" was certainly the case. Men with civic rights wore their elaborate civic gown, the toga, for formal occasions. Among the nobility, it was decorated with a narrow purple stripe

Monumental inscription, width 2.43 m, honouring Paternus Clementianus, governor of the neighbouring province of Noricum and his bust (original in Klagenfurt Museum). Ca. 130 AD; found at his place of residence in ABODIACVM = Epfach am Lech.

for relatives of knights, and a broad one for senators. It was thus identifiable from afar whom one was encountering in the streets; though, in AELIA AVGVSTA, relatives of the Roman aristocracy were very rare.

In Roman Augsburg at that time, people of completely different origins and social rank encountered one another: native Romanized Vindelici of Celtic descent, Italics with Roman civic rights, Germans who had settled at the edge of town, traders from the Western provinces, such as Galls or from the Danube provinces, even from the Orient or North Africa, relatives of administrators or soldiers at the governor's residence from all parts of the empire, citizens, freedmen and serfs. A hustle and bustle and multilingual babble of this melange of peoples must have filled the markets, the forum, the Roman baths, temples, streets and squares. Latin was the official written and spoken language for 400 years in Augsburg. Some public buildings have been archaeologically excavated, but largely eliminated or covered by modern building projects – that includes the Roman bath on Pettenkoferstraße and Georgenstraße, a more than 70-metre long market hall on Stephansgasse, or another Roman bath between Karmelitengasse and Äußeres Pfaffengässchen, at least a part of which, according to the recent study in 1999, should be marked in the planned park. The forum with basilica, which was used for official and legal transactions as well as for traders, was located in what is now "Stephansgarten", but has not been excavated.

In the city's heyday around 200 AD, we encounter, through inscriptions and stone reliefs, professional and cult associations, a pork dealer, the two Pompeianus brothers with their wine dealership and tavern (tomb from the Vorderer Lech), several tableware dealers and textile merchants, such as the purple dye trader Claudius Euphrates from the far Orient or, to mention the upper classes, the governor of 196/197 AD, C. Iulius Avitus Alexianus from Emesa in Syria, who, as brother-in-law of the Empress Iulia Domna, was related to the Emperor Septimius Severus. Foods were brought from near and far, as demonstrated by the picture of wine transportation on an ox-drawn cart from Heilig-Kreuz-Straße, the numerous oil am-

phoras from Southern Spain or individual date amphoras from Palestine. The farms from round about and some exclusively furnished villae rusticae, such as those in Stadtbergen and Friedberg, ensured basic supplies. The archaeological excavations also give evidence of a glass dealer on Jesuitengasse, a jewellery trade with gown pins from Gaul beneath the present-day administrative court, a lamp trader with oil lamps from Modena, but also a coin forger on Heilig-Kreuz-Straße. Testaments to crafts are the horseshoeing smithy at Fronhof, the glass blowers at Heilig-Kreuz-Straße and on Äußeres Pfaffengässchen (glass furnaces examined in 1999). Construction materials such as tuff, Jura limestone and wood were unloaded from the Lech barges and rafts at the "harbour", examined in 1994, close to the Vincentinum and "Fünffingerles-Turm", bricks from the workshops of Westheim or Stätzling were brought by coach. The extensive building trade can be seen in the excavated wooden and stone buildings, the fountains, gravel roads, the water pipes and sewers, the underfloor heating in houses and public buildings, roof tiles, but also the high-quality interior decoration with columns, marble cladding, wall frescos and coloured floor mosaics. AELIA AVGVSTA – a living ancient city as in Italy itself.

The "Roman" Augsburgers encountered the Gods at every corner and civic square. Wherever space permitted, there were altars, small chapel-like shrines, or even large temples. A capitol temple to Jupiter, Juno and Minerva – the triumvirate that headed the Roman pantheon must have stood at the forum, the central square of the city south of St. Stephan. Also worshipped were Mars and Victoria, Mercury, Apollo, Fortuna, Venus, Hercules, Diana, Vulcan, Pluto and Prosperpina, but also the Celtic Sucellus, the oriental godheads Bacchus, Cybele and Sol (Mithras) and Isis and Serapis from Egypt. In houses, in the lararium near the entrance – the devotional corner – one encountered the patron gods of house and family. Typical of worship is the votive formula "willingly, gladly and deservedly fulfilled a vow": The promise to build a temple or make a sacrifice was fulfilled as the godhead "deserved" after a received blessing. The fact that the god of merchants and money, Mercury, headed the hit list in terms of inscriptions, sculptures or bronze fig-

urines, underscores the provincial metropolis's central economic role – a presage of its later standing as the "Fugger city".

Encountering death was just as inescapable for the Romans as for us: But, in AELIA AVGVSTA, as throughout the Roman Empire, people were far more conspicuously confronted with it than today. That means that before the city gates, travellers had to pass by mile-wide stretches of graves, sites of funeral pyres, or elaborate tomb monuments alongside the arterial roads, making them direct witnesses to the funeral rites. The monuments were intended to keep alive the memory, and therefore the connection, to the living. They were therefore often erected while the subject was still alive, like the pillar of the legal scholar (pragmaticus) M. Aurelius Carus, recovered in 1998 at Hofer Straße in Oberhausen. Many stone tombs bear pictures of the deceased or reliefs of everyday life: purchasing wine, tying up textile bales, office and payment scenes – they had another function as publicity for the business. Almost without exception, they were crowned by pine cones, the symbol for survival in the beyond from the cult of Cybele. The pine cones often found in the middle ages are the reason why the "cedar nut", as the Augsburgers say, became the symbol and coat of arms of Augsburg from Renaissance times. Excavations of late-Roman inhumation graveyards around St. Ulrich and Afra or on Frölichstraße mean for archaeologists face-to-face "encounters" with the Romans interred there.

During the Empire's permanent internal crisis and with continual attacks by Germans, economic plight, fear and terror, pillaging and death were encountered by the residents of AELIA AVGVSTA from the mid-3rd century. An elegant testament is provided by the "Augsburg Victory Altar" from Gänsbühl (1992). Its text records a victory by the Romans supported by the citizenry, over the barbarian Juthungi (a Swabian tribe) on April 24/25, 260. With the subsequent eradication of the governor for treachery against the emperor, this Victoria Altar is Augsburg's most important record from Roman times! Even after the stabilization of the frontier of the province at the Danube, and stationing of more mounted troops, Augsburg was still not spared attacks by the Alemanni during the

4th century. But we still encounter the end of the "Roman" administration and dominance north of the Alps into the mid-5th century, with precious remains such as expensive glasses from Rome or "imports" such as tableware from North Africa, which indicate a degree of prosperity in AELIA AVGVSTA. Even in the late antiquity, it is visible that Germans were increasingly employed in the service of Rome to defend the frontiers and in the field army.

While there was a movement from cremation to inhumation during the 3rd century as a result of the increasing influence of oriental religions, the established Roman religions and Christianity, which was tolerated from 313, encountered one another during the 4th century. The "victory" of Christianity was completed towards the end of the 4th century, when the "heathen" temples were closed or even destroyed. This background makes it clear why almost all our stone deities are "headless", like the Mercury statues from the shrine on the VIA CLAVDIA in Gersthofen. The oldest "Christian" finding is a glass dish with picture of the Fall of Adam and Eve, made ca. 330/340 in the Cologne area, which was discovered in 2000 in "Hinter dem Schwalbeneck".

The encounters between Romans and Germans in the 3rd and 4th centuries were mainly warlike and had consequences. Despite all the efforts of the late-Roman emperor, the areas north of the Alps could no longer be "held" in the 5th century. The Alemanni took de facto dominance. The 5th and 6th centuries are still largely obscure to us. Traces of survival in the Roman ruins have been found in the latest excavations south of the Roman town around the Cathedral and at Schwalbeneck. The continuation of a Christian community with veneration of the martyr Afra, who according to legend was burnt on a Lech island in the early 4th century, is documented by Venantius Fortunatus for the time around 565: "If you are able to cross the barbarian rivers, so that you can peacefully pass over the Rhine and Danube, you arrive in Augsburg, where the Wertach and Lech flow. There you will worship the bones of the holy martyr Afra." Buried in the graveyard around St. Ulrich and Afra in the 7th century, "ad sanctos" lie the oldest clerics known in Augsburg. The "insignias" in the grave include a crozier or reliquary buckles. From the 8th century, bishops, starting with Wikterp, were also interred here until the late 10th century (Bishop Ulrich 973), to a certain extent continuing the Roman metropolis of Augsburg as a spiritual centre. The centre of the Christian faith was the Cathedral, consecrated in the Carolingian year of 807 under Bishop Simpert. The oldest building remains, examined in 1998/99, can now be seen in the diocesan museum of St. Afra. The Roman stone ruins were almost entirely exploited as a "mediaeval quarry" until the 11th/12th century.

And we still encounter the Roman "legacy" in Augsburg at every step: in the city name and coat of arms, in the internationally used Roman alphabet, in the stone architecture "imported" by the Romans, and in the money economy, in the infrastructure of a city through to the water supply and drainage, in the public health system and baths to the sauna and hot-air floor heating, in the bequeathed Christian religion and in Roman law, but also in the reused ashlars and monuments in the cathedral, at the tower of the Heilig-Kreuz church, the Barfüßerkirche or the "Sieben-Kindl stone". Architectural elements, sculptures and inscriptions can be found exhibited on the "Roman wall" in front of the Cathedral, and opposite as a collection at "Peutinger House" on Peutingerstraße, where the famous Augsburg humanist and founder of the current Roman research lived (1465–1547). In the courtyard there, the grave inscription of Iulianus Iulius is carved into the wall, an aedile in the early 3rd century and therefore one of the key figures in Roman city administration.

The Roman roots of this city are ineradicable. At Domplatz itself, the foundations of a large Roman Italianate peristyle house have been on display since late 1999 beneath the wall remains of the Carolingian church of St. John, which is conserved there. A direct encounter with Roman buildings, roads and city walls is still a vision: At Am Pfannenstiel, we have a unique chance to excavate an entire district of AELIA AVGVSTA with the northern city wall, and conserve sections of it as an "archaeological park". Then, encounters with Roman Augsburg could be experienced just as intensely as in Trier, Cologne or Mainz, the other Roman provincial capitals on German soil!

Carnelian cameo showing a fishing satyr on the back of the goat-fish Capricorn, the zodiac sign of Augustus; width 1.95 cm. 1st century BC; Jesuitengasse, 1990.

Gilded officers' or guards' helmets of the 4th century AD, from Pfersee, 1897.

Glass dish with scratched ornamentation showing the Fall of Adam and Eve. Inscription: VIVAS IN DEO P(ie) Z(eseis) = Live in God. Drink. Thou willst Live! CA. 330/340 AD.

Victoria altar commemorating a major Roman victory over Germanic Juthungi on April 24/25, 260, consecrated on 11th September, 260 AD. Jura limestone, height 1.64 m; from Gänsbühl, 1992.

Excavation of a child's grave with ceramic and glass offerings from the first half of the 4th century AD in the graveyard on Frölichstraße, 1985.

Early Christian reliquary buckle from a whalebone, with picture of the miracle of Jonah. Early 7th century AD; made in southern France. Crypt of St. Ulrich and Afra, grave 9, 1961.

AUGSBURG'S AGE OF GLORY

The age of the Fugger and Welser families, the period of Emperor Maximilian, is always celebrated as the epoch of "golden Augsburg". This may refer to the city's economic power at that time, and to the fabulous wealth of the rich merchant princes; but above all it reflects the glory of art. It is the era of Holbein, of Jörg Breu, Hans Burgkmeier, of the sculptor Gregor Erhart and the goldsmith Jörg Seld. At that time, between the mid-15th century and the famous Diet of 1555, Augusta was at the peak of its glory. With perhaps 30,000 inhabitants, it was one of the largest cities in the Holy Roman Empire, and considered by some visitors as also its finest. But let us first go back to the beginnings.

A millennium before this, following the fall of the Western Roman Empire, no one could have predicted such a future for this small patch of ground on the river Lech. The ancestors of today's Augsburgers had probably settled in a makeshift way among the ancient city ruins, now much too big. The walls of Roman Augusta surrounded the early mediaeval Augsburgers like a cloak too big for a body grown thin. The turmoil of the mass migrations had resulted in a deep fracture. The church emerged as the law enforcer very early on, and the bishops as the actual rulers of the city. They were not only spiritual leaders, but had the last word on almost everything, including military matters. Bishop

Ulrich – later one of the city saints alongside Afra and Sintpert – organised the defence of Augsburg in advance of the bloody battle on Lechfeld in 955. The Imperial Army under Emperor Otto I won a decisive victory over the Hungarians, who had been threatening large parts of eastern and southern Germany until then.

Augsburg owed its important standing in the mediaeval Empire to its favourable strategic location as "gateway to the south". The Lechfeld, soaked in Hungarian blood, was where the armies of German kings and emperors mustered on their march to Italy; Augsburg accommodated nearly all the important rulers of the Middle Ages in its walls. Thus the city strengthened its ties to the monarchy, a circumstance that was to become of crucial importance in its acquisition of Imperial Immediacy.

We know little about what Augsburg looked like up to the turn of the millennium. A biography of St. Ulrich and archaeological findings suggest that the old Roman city, i.e. principally the Cathedral quarter, still formed the core of the settlement. Another nucleus was the

Cityscape by Michael Wolgemut, Wilhelm Pleydenwurff and Workshop. Coloured woodcut from the richly illustrated Schedel's World Chronicle, 1493, Nuremberg (Kunstsammlungen und Museen Augsburg).

grave of St. Afra, where St. Ulrich's basilica is to be found now. This was where Benedictine monks settled. The two centres were connected by a road that approximately followed the ancient Via Claudia, and traced the course of Maximilianstraße and Karolinenstraße. Half way along it was a small hill that the documents call "Perleich" – "Perlach" – where merchants and traders apparently settled. A market must have grown up here over time; around the year 1000, where the town hall and Perlach tower will one day stand, we can imagine a few meagre clay-daubed and thatched wooden houses. To the north east of the Episcopal city, Ulrich founded a convent near to the church dedicated to St. Stephen. The importance that this city on the river Lech had gained by now can be seen by the fact that, at the end of the tenth century, its bishop had to provide one hundred knights in armour for the Imperial Army. Augsburg thus ranked among the three most important episcopal cities of the Ottonian Empire. From the 11th century, Augsburg population grew rapidly. There are many historical references to this trend, which can be observed throughout Europe. At any rate, in the area around the city, numerous new settlements were established or existing settlements expanded. The sources mention towns such as Chrechesaver, Pherresee or Liutericheshoven – rustic-sounding names, which are nevertheless familiar to well-informed locals; and even strangers can quickly find on the map. Today they are the suburbs Kriegshaber, Pfersee and Leitershofen.

In Augsburg itself, increasing numbers of stone buildings probably arose around that time. The settlements around St. Afra and Perlach, and surrounding the episcopal city gradually merged. In 1065, Bishop Embrico was able to consecrate a cathedral, erected in the modern Romanesque style. Other church buildings during the 11th and 12th centuries testify to the growing economic power of the episcopal city: St. Gallus (the small church was consecrated by a genuine pope, Leo IX), St. Martin, St. Peter am Perlach, St. Moritz (St. Maurice). Even Saints Ulrich and Afra received fine new churches. This region was included in the city fortifications by no later than the second half of the 12th century; another suburb arose below Perlachberg.

In the Investiture Controversy, the Augsburgers took the Emperor's side: the danger was that the opposition bishop, who was loyal to the Pope, was allied with the Bavarian Welfen. This duchy across the Lech remained a disagreeable, sometimes threatening, neighbour of the Swabian city. In the conflict between the Staufer and Welfen, the Augsburg citizenry took the side of the Staufer family, while its Bishop sided with the Welfen. Over time, the Metropolis Sueviae, "the metropolis of Swabia" (according to the chronicler Ekkehard von Aura) became one of the most important pillars of Staufer power. Barbarossa often stayed in Augsburg. In 1156, he issued a document to the Augsburgers – the so-called Justitia Civitatis Augustensis, which shows that the Bishop still held control. Only the outline of an independent civic legal sphere can be seen. However, the Emperor gained rights and extensive property in and around Augsburg. A second bailiff employed by the ruler officiated as governor. Staufer occasionally spoke of the Augsburgers as "his beloved citizens": Augsburg gradually emerged as a royal city.

Incidentally, the powerful Staufers had a document drawn up within the Augsburg city walls on June 14, 1158, which regulated a local dispute that, in itself, was trivial. It dealt with a conflict between Heinrich der Löwe and the Monastery of Freising; the Welfe had razed a market town, Veringen, which had been unlawfully established on the Isar. In its stead, he created a new market a little further south: Munichen. Barbarossa's document ensured the continuation of this market. The first documented reference to what was to become the glitzy metropolis of Munich, now Augsburg's overpowering rival, can thus be found in a document prepared in Augsburg. You could almost say that Munich was founded in Augsburg.

Augsburg under the Staufers saw glorious days: in 1197, Philipp von Schwaben became engaged to the Byzantine Emperor's daughter Irene; Friedrich II held court assemblies, at which the Augsburgers were awed by the Staufer's exotic entourage, which contemporaries called a "wonder of the world": Saracens and negroes, who guarded his valuables, monkeys, leopards and camels.

The sources cast a spotlight on a bustling day-to-day life: we learn, for example, that the Augsburgers could afford to drink not only beer, milk and mead, but also Greek wine; There are also regulations governing the weight of bread (for a given price). A doctor, Master Albertus, cared for the sick. At the same time, a "social infrastructure" grew up: The Holy Spirit Spital (which now houses the Augsburger Puppenkiste) was founded between 1239 and 1245, at St. Servatius, a lepers' house was built, and mendicant orders – Franciscans and Dominicans – settled here. Around the mid-13th century, Beguine communities arose, "women's communes" who cared for the sick and were active in the education of young ladies. From 1212, there is also evidence of a Jewish community in Augsburg.

The civic community gradually emerges from the twilight of the records. The names of some families, who later form the core of the patricians, are named in the sources. Stolzhirsch, for example, or Welser. An important date in Augsburg's constitutional history is 1237. This is the year of the oldest city seal, a symbol of the Civium Augustensium, the citizens of Augsburg. But it was to take some decades still before the Episcopal city government could be shaken off and Augsburg gained Imperial Immediacy. In the Augsburg civic law of 1276, the Bishop is still to be found alongside the king as city ruler. This law book is of interest not only as a document of constitutional history (it is the second oldest civic law in Germany) – but is also a treasure trove for

Hector Mülich, probably the oldest representation of Augsburg, coloured pen-and-ink drawing by Sigismund Meisterlin, 1457 (Kunstsammlungen und Museen Augsburg).

vnd des iars ward gemacht hie an diser statt die mull
vo wertachpruck vn wurden die pruggen allenthalbn
vor den toren gewelbt vn das ratthaus gar gemacht
mit dem turnlin dan vor aussen an dem rautthaus vm
ain holtzin gang was vn ain hultzin turnlin da die glock
in hieng vnd beschach nach cristi gepurt M xii lxiij°
vn des iars zu miterfasten ward michel rem ainbur
ger hie erstochen vo ainem vo strassburg von feint
schaft wegen die er zu im hett beschach an d' lechpruck

Nach criftÿ gepurt · 1500 · iar Was dife claidung zu dugfpurg das ift war ·

everyone interested in everyday life in a late-mediaeval city. At the "Huckers", the Augsburgers bought all kinds of foods, such as eels, sturgeons and figs; the "Huenraer" sold game, poultry, cheese and fat. The goldsmiths' trade, later to become world renowned, is also mentioned. And there are insights into the topography. For example, the Lech canals are mentioned, the arteries of the craftsmen's quarter that spreads out at the foot of the high terrace – sources of energy for the hammer mills and corn millers, essential funds of raw materials for the tanners, furriers and dyers. And they were a convenient way of disposing of used tanning liquor, raw sewage, and all kinds of refuse that the old city produced en masse. Anyone who idealises the "good old days" should know that this was a foul-smelling age.

This, like all mediaeval cities, horribly stinking Augsburg had by now become an international trading metropolis. Its merchants could be found in Flanders and at fairs in the Champagne. They traded in textiles, pre-

cious substances, spices, glass and cotton from Venice. The trading network will one day support "golden Augsburg" is already emerging.

The growing economic power of the civic city appears as an important condition for its rise to Imperial Immediacy. A crucial factor was the weakness of central power after the fall of the House of Staufer. Rudolf von Habsburg and other kings and emperors bestowed rights and privileges on Augsburg to assure its support. While battling the Habsburg Friedric der Schöne (Frederick the Handsome), who was supported by the Bishop of Augsburg, Emperor Ludwig der Bayer confirmed Augsburg's inalienability from the Empire "forever", since the city "stands out as a respectable and excellent city among the cities of the Empire". "imperial city" –

Heinrich Vogtherr d. J. (?), Perlach Square ca. 1540, framed by the city butcher, Perlach Tower and Gothic Town Hall (Kunstsammlungen und Museen Augsburg).

that means that the Augsburgers would never again be subject to princes, but only the Emperor, the Empire and God would rule over them. Augsburg's constitution remained "republican", although there were several attempts to stage rebellions and erect "tyrannies" on the Italian model. Thus, the patrician Siboto Stolzhirsch – his name, "proud stag", speaks for itself – tried to seize power for his clan and followers through violence. But the plot was discovered, and the plotters fled or had to do penance. In 1349, an attempted rebellion by Portner failed.

After the Stolzhirsch putsch, a constitutional structure developed, which in outline was to last for a long time. The fate of the city was determined by a small and a large council; at the head were two "Stadtpfleger". From a group of four councillors, who surrounded them, there grew up over time the secret council which developed into the actual power centre of the imperial city. The favourable economic development was slowed in the first half of the 14th century, partly by the agricultural crisis that seized large parts of Europe and was associated with a worsening in the climate, and partly by plagues, of which the Black Death from 1346/50 has gained a grim renown. Georgsvorstadt was walled around and Jakober Vorstadt was also walled in 1339; at that time, Augsburg must have had around 15,000 inhabitants, including the city poor, clerics, Jews and other outsiders. It was not until the mid-19th century that the corset set around Augsburg at this time became too tight.

We know little about how the plague affected Augsburg. However, here, too, there were Jewish pogroms: "Anno 1349 jar… verprant man die juden zuo Augspurg" ("In 1349 … the Jews in Augsburg were burned") reports one chronicle. Shuddering citizens also witnessed processions of flagellants, men who thrashed one another's backs bloody to elicit God's mercy through this chastisement. In the Jews, the Augsburgers found scapegoats, guilty parties for the otherwise inexplicable visitation by the plague. Those who survived the persecution settled in the vicinity of Augsburg, some even directly in front of the city gates in Kriegshaber or Steppach.

The plague epidemics and agricultural crisis led to a rural exodus; in the cities there was a shifting of wealth, since the money of the dead was left to the living. The elaborate rebuilding of the Cathedral, whose choir rose to Gothic heights in 1356, must perhaps be seen against this sombre background: by building chapels and altars and founding masses, the citizens were investing in their spiritual welfare.

There is little doubt that the crafts emerged strengthened from the crisis of the 14th century. In the cities, there was a lack of skilled artisans; while the reduced population caused a collapse in agricultural prices; the late 14th century was an important epoch for crafts. No wonder then that the craftsmen organised in guilds soon demanded political rights. The troubles of 1368, known with some exaggeration as the "guilds revolution", must be seen in this context. According to one chronicler, many people armed themselves and gathered on Perlach, demanding a share of power. The rebellion was bloodless; the old elites conceded. Augsburg was now ruled by the guilds for almost two hundred years. But the victors cleverly also shared power with the patricians.

As a powerful member of the Swabian league of cities, Augsburg managed to preserve its status as an imperial city. In the 15th century, the city steered a careful course of foreign policy, apart from its involvement in the "Margrave War" around the middle of the century. Augsburg now became a major protagonist on the stage of the European economy. The connections of the big commercial dynasties, with the Welser and Fugger families at their head, now extended from the Atlantic to the Mediterranean.

But the crises hadn't ended. They were the result of Augsburg's economic monostructure: the fate of the civic economy depended on the development of the textile market; even at that time, weaving was by far the most important craft in the Imperial City. Market crises

had a backlash on the living conditions of a large proportion of the citizenry. Actually the economic boom faltered somewhat between 1440 and 1470. Textile production declined from about 1440; even the big financiers apparently suffered losses. Against the background of growing social tension, the powerful guild mayor Ulrich Schwarz tried to seize power. He paid with his life. In 1478, he died on the gallows after only two years' rule.

The 15th century was a major building epoch. The construction of a major town hall had already begun in 1385. The dance house at St. Moritz (demolished in 1632) became the civic social centre; building work on the Ulrich Basilica began in 1474. They started paving the streets at last. The façades of the patrician palaces were decorated with coloured frescos modelled on buildings in Northern Italy. A contemporary observer at the beginning of the 16th century regarded the Fugger House as the finest palace in Germany. It was also the Fugger dynasty who imported the first Renaissance art into Augsburg. The glory of "golden Augsburg" is illuminated by the light of Italy. The great Augsburg printer Erhard Ratdolf imported a magnificent antique document from Venice; the city on the Lech became one of the most important printing centres of the Holy

Hans Holbein the Elder,
Votive Picture of Ulrich Schwarz and His Family, 1508
(Kunstsammlungen und Museen Augsburg).

Roman Empire. Augsburg printers crossed the Alps to familiarise themselves with the avant garde there. The aging Hans Holbein must also have been acquainted with the art of Italy.

At the same time, they began examining the city's history. Roman origins were not enough to satisfy the Augsburgers' pride: some chroniclers placed Augsburg's foundation in the time immediately after the great Flood, and so shifted it back to the very beginning of history. In his annals, the doctor Achilles Pirmin Gasser told a story in which Augsburg had even been founded twice. In grey prehistory, "600 years before Rome was built" the Amazon queen Marthesia, ruler of a wild race of warlike women, conquered the postdiluvian Augsburg and razed it to the ground; as occupying force, the heroin left behind "several wild, vicious women", of whom, the author maliciously adds, there are many still living in Augsburg.

In the Augsburg reality of the 16th century, events started happening very fast. The influence of the reformation started to make itself felt. Luther's teachings spread rapidly partly thanks to the Augsburg printers. The Fugger family became the most important pillar of the Old Catholic faith in Augsburg.

Now, as in the long-past Staufer age, Renaissance Augsburg appears to be at the centre of imperial politics. The sociable Emperor Maximilian had visited the city of the Fuggers, his bankers, so often that he was derided as the "Mayor of Augsburg". His grandson Emperor Charles V also spent time in the city now and again. The 16th century saw some glorious Diets in Augsburg's walls. In 1518, when Luther was interrogated by the papal legate Cajetan; in 1530, when the Confession of Faith was handed to Charles V, which the religious community from then on gave the name "Confessio Augusta"; in 1547/48, when Charles V, after his victory over the Schmalkadic League, appeared to be lord over the Empire and the Imperial City; and finally in 1555, when the epochal Peace of Augsburg was signed. After that, the Augsburg Confession was for the first time legally recognised throughout the Holy Roman Empire; but the respective sovereign still determined the faith of his subjects. In Augsburg, a community with two confessions emerged. The philosopher Michel de Montaigne, who visited Augsburg in 1580, was amazed at how peacefully the religious groups lived together. In France, with the Bartholomew's night massacre and the religious civil war, things were different!

Nevertheless, the second half of the 16th century was not a happy time for the great majority of Augsburgers. The "Little Ice Age", which had made itself felt on the Lech since the 1560s, led to famines and impoverished wide strata of society. In Augsburg, too, there were hunts for witches as the supposed font of all evil; but it was only in the 17th century that there were executions. Here, the city had the power to realise a major programme of art and architecture: the series of ceremonial fountains and many buildings, with Elias Holl's town hall as the pinnacle. Only now had Augsburg really become a Renaissance city.

Despite its uncertainties and defects, the Peace of 1555 gave the Empire and Augsburg the longest period of peace in its history until now. That is easily forgotten, since the long shadow of the Thirty Year War falls over it, which for Augsburg was an absolute catastrophe. Hunger and plague reaped a rich harvest; the nadir was reached in 1634/35, when the city was besieged by an Imperial-Bavarian Army and starved out. It is said that the distraught people even fed on human flesh – cannibalism in Augsburg!

Only a few German cities were hit so hard by the war. Around 1618, there were around 40-45,000 residents in Augsburg; a census taken shortly before the end of the war recorded just 16,000 souls. The worst affected were the poor. The weaving trade, in which a few thousand people had worked around 1600 only counted a few hundred master weavers. When peace was signed in 1648, Augsburg achieved parity: both confessions were now guaranteed their right to exist in the city. The citizens came to terms with the parity system as well as they could. During the war, where city was first to be re-Catholicised, and then briefly came under Swedish, i.e. Protestant, control, they had found out how dangerous religious fanaticism could be. Migration from the surrounding countryside gradually turned Augsburg, once a symbol of Lutherism, into a predominantly Catholic community.

The Thirty Year War meant an economic and cultural hiatus, from which the city was never to recover. Augsburg's status as the European economic metropolis had gone forever. People invested in luxury crafts. Augsburg goldsmithery reached the zenith of its importance. Augsburg copperplate engravings were to be found all over the world, Augsburg also managed to become a significant publishing location again – but only in terms of quantity, not the quality of literary production.

The weight shifted to the cities with royal residences; Munich, too, outstripped its rival on the Lech. In fact, the great majority of Augsburgers saw it as an opportunity when, in 1806, the last hour struck for the imperial city and it was incorporated into the State of Bavaria.

THE FUGGER CITY

"Can it serve a divine and rightful purpose if a man become so rich in such a short time that he contemplates buying kings and emperors?" The reformer Martin Luther, from whom this quotation originates, was probably not the only one who was surprised at the meteoric rise of the Augsburger Fugger family, and its patron at the time, Jakob Fugger the Wealthy (1459–1525). The star of the Fuggers stood like a comet – astonishingly fast, visible from afar and golden – over the Imperial City. Many an Augsburger must have looked up in a mixture of respect and astonishment at the oriel of the golden orderly room by the cattle market, which he would never be able to enter, but from which were spun the golden threads of a commercial empire that held sway over not only Augsburg's everyday history. And the name of the Fuggers was on everyone's lips. "These Fuggers are now the greatest business-men in the whole of Christendom", wrote the traveller Antonio de Beatis in 1517.

Money – power – art – faith: four pillars of the Fugger commercial empire and its great strategist Jakob Fugger.

Jakob Fugger the Wealthy himself stressed that his own rise and that of his house took place by the grace of God. His grandfather Hans had migrated into the Imperial City from the nearby Lechfeld, attracted, like so many others, by the towers of the city on the Lech, visible from afar and holding out promise of betterment. Hans Fugger appears in a tax ledger entry of 1367. Earlier researchers had him as penniless, but Hans Fugger by no means came to Augsburg without means. There, thanks to a favorable marriage and skilful management, he rapidly rose to become a master weaver. In 1396, he had reached 41st place (of 2930) in the hierarchy of the city taxpayers. A year later, he possessed a well-situated house. The cornerstone of the Fugger trading house had been laid, but the house had not yet been built.

Even Martin Luther conjures up the image of the money king Fugger whose hands adroitly intervened in the early-modern mesh of economics and politics. But the other side was also soon to emerge. Those who pull the strings can also be pulled themselves. The House of Fugger's connections to the Habsburgs was both beneficial and destructive. It was a substantial factor in the rise of this Augsburg dynasty, but was also responsible for their economic waning. However, from around the mid-16th century, decline can only be spoken of in economic terms. The Fuggers continued to play important roles, as politicians, in military service, on their country estates, or not least as patrons.

Martin Luther emphasized the rapid rise of the House of Fugger, but we must not overlook the fact that the rise by no means directly affected Jakob Fugger the Wealthy and his nephew Anton (1493–1560), under whose auspices the wealth of the House reached its zenith. However, Anton, recognising the signs of the times, gave the family politics a new orientation towards land ownership.

The bankruptcy of the Fugger vom Reh family towards the end of the 15th century can well be seen as a warning shadow over the account books of the "Fugger von der Lilie" branch of the family. One could achieve a lot through loans, for example receive benefits and privileges; but what if the loan can no longer be paid back.

The success for the family with the lily on their coat of arms was huge. In 1511, they were included in the imperial nobility, a little later in the earldom. In 1538, with the substantial expansion of the patricians, they rose to the city nobility. In addition, numerous financial concessions must be mentioned, made to them by the Habsburgs as their chief debtors. However, in their financial heyday, the Fuggers succeeded in leading the dance at several weddings. There was no shortage of cash-hungry courts, from whose contacts the Fuggers could profit in turn. They shuffled the cards vigorously in the commercial nerve centres, in Antwerp, in the ailing Venice, in Lisbon and Lyons, but they never staked everything on one card. Augsburg money was worth something in the world, and the Fuggers' wealth was legendary.

Fugger business policy was focused on banking, the real estate leaseholds of the Spanish Orders of Santiago, Alcántara and Calatrava (Maestrazgos), mining in Hungary and, of declining importance, Tyrolean mining. From Augsburg, a network of establishments was cast across Europe, America, India and Africa. These remote feelers, so-called "factories", were the extended arms of the commercial empire "at the coal face", so to speak. From these establishments, rare animals were brought to Augsburg, which stocked the Fugger zoo in the 16th century. But economic, social and political news also proceeded from the establishments to the Augsburg headquarters in the form of the Fugger newspapers, in the second half of the 16th century. Some people made remarkable careers from the factories, like other employees of the tight-knitted empire.

The economic success was manifested in the Augsburg city architecture. In 1511/1512, Jakob Fugger acquired a double property on the wine market – now Maximilianstraße. Further purchases and rebuilding measures, continuing after Jakob's death, resulted in a High-German/Italian city palace with a façade measuring almost 70 metres along the eaves, which used to be decorated with frescos by the Renaissance painter Hans Burgkmair. Even today, it still gives the street a face in the truest sense of the word. Many travellers praised the qualitative and quantitative uniqueness of the Fugger palace. Behind its

In its day, the Fugger Palace saw some great guests. It is famous for its beautiful courtyards, like the Serenadenhof shown here and, most famous and finest of all, the Damenhof (preceding page).

large façade are three courtyards, of which the trapezoidal Damenhof (Ladies' Court) is particularly important in art history as one of the earliest Renaissance accomplishments north of the Alps.

Under the roof of the city palace, formerly covered with Hungarian copper – there was even talk that the Fuggers would have had it roofed with gold, if they had been allowed to – there was a room known as the palatium, intended for eminent guests such as the king or emperor. And they visited comparatively often, in the case of Maximilian I and his grandson Charles V. With the former, Jakob Fugger had extremely lucrative business contacts. The result was mining shares in Tyrol, Kärnten, Thuringia or Hungary. In addition, there was the classical trade in Augsburg's traditional products, fustian – a mixed cloth – but also cinnabar, silver, in some cases gold, mercury and other Italian, Spanish and imports from overseas. At this time, almost all roads led to Augsburg, but also from Augsburg, which profited from its strategic geographic location. And the Fuggers' trademark of the trident crossed the world. Matthäus Schwarz, accountant at the Augsburg headquarters for many generations of Fuggers, recorded the business impeccably, and to the latest standards of double-entry bookkeeping.

The Fuggers' influence in the financial transaction of the St. Peter indulgences and the election of the King in 1519 reached spectacular and celebrated dimensions. Jakob raised 850,000 guilders for it, 543,585 from the coffers of his bank. The "sweeteners" probably went a long way towards facilitating the decision of the prince electors; though accusations of bribery as understood in the modern

age are probably out of place. The outstanding monetary obligations alone must have stimulated Jakob's interest in the election of a Habsburg. At any rate, Charles V was elected, and eleven years later was crowned emperor by the Pope, as the last in a centuries-old tradition. Rejoicing and jubilations were not only to be heard in Augsburg. The ties between the Fuggers and Habsburgs were drawn even tighter. And Jakob knew the significance of what he had done: "It is also widely known and open, that your Royal Majesty could not have acquired the Roman crown without my help", he wrote to the Emperor Charles V.

In an age characterised by a religious hunger that can scarcely be overestimated, the Fuggers incurred the wrath of reformationist circles, for example for the scarcely religiously justifiable sale of indulgences, which they were involved in for a long time – for example for the construction of the Augsburg Dominican Church. Luther raged, and Ulrich von Hutten, crowned poeta laureatus in Augsburg drew his pen against the allegedly illegitimate financial baron. We do Jakob an injustice if we judge him by modern business practices. It is equally wrong to put his dealings into late-mediaeval and modern compartments. This is to separate what, in Fugger's own view belongs together.

Jakob's world view united the external and internal. Piety was not a private matter; it both legitimated and obligated. The monetary dealings with the Papal State resulted in synergy effects for commerce but also for the church careers of family members. By financing 150 Swiss mercenaries, the Fuggers laid a cornerstone of the Papal private army, the Swiss Guard. But contemporaries also saw the modernity that was associated with the Fuggers. Some years after Jakob Fugger and Ambrosius Höchstetter had carved up the European copper market, and thereby set up the first local cartel for copper in economic history, an animated dispute broke out about the permissibility of monopolies. Some complaints struck at the high walls of the Fugger palace, but ultimately Charles V decided in favour of the trading houses.

And the Fuggers gave back to the city from which they had profited so abundantly. The famous "Fuggerei", the oldest public housing

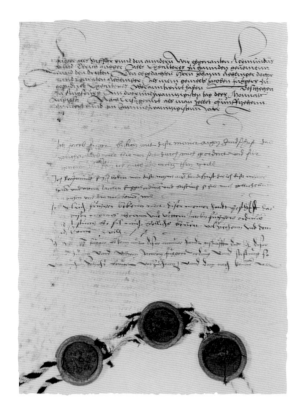

estate in the world, founded in 1514, is committed to the idea of memoria in two ways: firstly in providing for the welfare of their own soul, and secondly in an effort to ensure a spiritual legacy in the varied social structure of the age. And he succeeded in this. Thus, the dramatist Barthold von Gadenstedt wrote at the end of the 16th century: "Die hern fuckarten haben auch den rhum, das sie den armen viel guts thun." (The Fugger lords also have the reputation of doing much good for the poor). The deed of endowment of Jakob Fugger of 1521, now kept in the Fugger archive in Dillingen, sees a relationship between the Fuggerei, intended to help the poor day labourers and craftsmen and the chapel in the Carmelite monastery of St. Anna. "To the glory of God and in thankfulness for the success shown in our trading in temporal goods," so begins the deed of endowment.

Above the Ox Gate, visitors to the Fuggerei see a Latin inscription which, beneath the year 1519, underlines the social aspect of the Fuggerei foundation. Bono reipublicae, to the welfare of the Augsburg community, this estate with its 106 residences has been founded. The endowment deed also specifies the course of prayers that the residents of the Fuggerei have been required to say to this very day for the founders and benefactors. A Pater Noster,

an Ave Maria, and a Credo. As annual rent, the deed of endowment proposed one rhenish guilder, to be paid in two annual instalments. Today, the approximately 150 Fuggerei residents pay a rent of 88 cent excluding heating costs, as a symbolic equivalent of the guilder (= 1.72 deutschmarks). But it should be mentioned that at the time of Jakob Fugger the Wealthy, a rhenish guilder had a much higher value and was roughly the weekly wage of a day labourer.

The Fuggerei, which still doesn't receive any state or church subsidies, grew over time to a total of 67 houses with 140 apartments. From 1580 to 1582, St. Mark's chapel was built. After it was partly destroyed by bombs in 1944, it was rebuilt and extended. The Schneidhaus Foundation, founded by Anton Fugger, in which the renowned Occo family of doctors practised, was one of the earliest private surgeries in Europe, In the Holzhaus, syphilitics were treated with Guiacum wood essences, which the Fuggers imported with their generally rather sporadically operated overseas trade. One of the roughly 60 square metre apartments was inhabited by Franz Mozart between 1681 and 1693, grandfather of the Augsburger Leopold Mozart and great grandfather of Wolfgang Amadeus.

The other side of the foundation coin, the Fugger chapel in St. Anna, dates back to 1509. It was consecrated in 1418 after the finest artists of the age, Albrecht Dürer, Sebastian Loscher, Hans Daucher and Jörg Breu, had collaborated on the funeral chapel. It is the earliest and most exquisite monument of the German Renaissance, in which probably Florentine models received an independent High German shape. The Fugger lilies crop up in many places, on the floor or in the ceiling rosette with the keystone showing the Mother of God. On the rear wall are epitaphs for the three brothers Ulrich, Georg and Jakob. Splendour and wealth were displayed before their fellow creatures, but also justified before God.

In 1494, those three brothers has signed a so-cial contract for six years at first, with which they agreed that the capital and profits gained would be kept with the firm. After the death of Georg in 1506 and the oldest of the three brothers, Ulrich, Jakob was entitled to con-tinue the business alone from 1510. Jakob's nephews committed themselves to obedience and to keep their fortune with the society in the event that their uncle remained childless, which actually was the case. And this fortune grew and grew. In 1516, Jakob was able to make a contract with the city of Augsburg which obliged him to pay a lump sum tax, but relieved him of the obligation to dis-close the exact value of his fortune to the tax officials.

The Dürer portrait of Jakob in the Augsburg state gallery, canvas on pinewood, shows the company head in a fur coat and with a Venet-ian cap, a reminder of Jakob's education and activities. In the days when the brothers head-ed the firm, he was responsible for the Augs-burg – Innsbruck – Venice axis. He gazes into the distance. Similarly, the older researchers made Jakob into an economic visionary with a extraordinary sense of what was economical-ly feasible and lucrative. More recent studies have shed light on this somewhat idealized mage by emphasizing the circumstances of the time and comparable careers. However, Jakob's extremely impressive farsightedness remains – alongside something that is hardly ever raised– the luck of the Fuggers.

Jakob, on whose death the chroniclers claimed to have seen portentous celestial phe-

nomena, left the fortune to his nephew Anton, son of his brother Georg. Anton, who headed the company autocratically, like a monarch, strengthened the company's key position. The Fugger – Habsburg financial axis still held. For the election of Ferdinand I in 1531, the Fuggers, who had already helped him succeed to the thrones of Hungary and Bohemia, once again raised large sums. The story of Augsburg increasingly became the story of the Reformation, and also included the House of Fugger. After the death of Jakob, his widow Sybilla Fugger, née Arzt, married the protestant patrician Konrad Rehlinger and was converted, which caused quite a storm. The Fuggers remained staunchly faithful to the old church, even though Augsburg was for the most part protestant.

Anton's brother Raymund, whose descendants formed the "Raymund line", had to be interred in secrecy in the Fugger chapel. An event five years before in the Fugger's family church, St. Maurice (St. Moritz), had raised angry furrows on the brows of the Protestant Augsburgers. St. Maurice, together with the Fuggerei and the burial chapel, formed the trinity of the Fugger foundation. On Ascension Day, Anton, following an old custom, had a figure of Christ raised in the church interior against the will of the parishioners. After the Fuggers had left, the figure was smashed down to the floor of the church to roars of anger. The dispute was to have far-reaching implications.

In the great religious dispute of the Schmalkaldic War of 1546 and 1547, the imperial city of Augsburg fought in the Protestant alliance against the imperial head Charles V, who was financially supported by Anton Fugger. It was the year in which the Fugger fortune was at its peak, but to a large extent consisted of unredeemed claims. The Habsburgers emerged winners from the war. An Augsburg delegation had to kneel before the Emperor in Ulm, Anton Fugger among them. The social-political split with one foot with the Emperor and the other in the imperial city became apparent in a symbolic way. Charles V came in triumph to Augsburg, staying in the Fugger palace, where Titian painted his famous portraits. But the elaborate Fugger network began to split in some places. Anton restructured it.

With wisdom and foresight, Anton – whom the Florentine Lodovico Guicciardini, who also worked in Antwerp, later called "truly the prince among other businessmen" (principe veramente degl'altri mercatanti) – acquired an array of estates: Babenhausen in 1538 and Kirchheim in 1551, both now in the district of Unterallgäu. The dark clouds began to gather in the once so bright Fugger heavens. The Hungarian possessions had long been suffering from declining profits, but the political situation, too, was beset by unrest and Ottoman incursions. Economic insecurity began to spread. The national bankruptcy of the House of Habsburg in 1557 pulled the Fugger company down with it, but didn't destroy it. At the same time, King Philipp of Spain, son of Charles V, could not be persuaded to repay his debts. It is therefore not surprising that Anton urged his successors to withdraw from commercial dealings. But this was to take another century.

Anton himself, who also remembered domestic servants and kitchen maids in his will, was laid to rest not in the now-Protestant church of St. Anna, beside his great uncle, in the Catholic Fugger Chapel, which is still private ground, but preferred to be buried in St. Andrew's Church of his country seat in Babenhausen. Anton's successors and relations also no longer wanted to be buried in St. Andrew's Church. Some are at rest in the total of five Fugger burial chapels in the former Benedictine church of St. Ulrich and Afra in Augsburg, where the extended Fugger organ reminds us of the family's musical patronage. Masters such as Giovanni Gabrieli, Hans Leo Hassler or Orlando di Lasso dedicated works to this Augsburg family. In the Georg chapel, a side epitaph of 1575 commemorates the deceased Johann Jakob Fugger, son of Anton's brother Raymund, a politician, humanist and art collector, who had to sell his famous library to the Bavarian Duke Albrecht V in 1571. Now this intellectual inheritance between book covers forms a valuable foundation of the Bavarian State Library. Johann Jakob is also commemorated by the only monument to a member of the House of Fugger in Augsburg, founded in 1857 by the abdicated Bavarian King Ludwig I. Other valuable holdings from the Fugger libraries can now be found in Vienna or Rome.

Another event that was largely facilitated by the Fuggers gained extensive importance, namely the settlement of the Jesuits in Augsburg in 1580, who built the very significant College of St. Salvator and a corresponding school. The works of the Societas Jesu in Augsburg are recalled by the Jesuitengasse and the Kleiner Goldener Saal. Gradually, the Fuggers continued along the road trodden by Anton. As country gentry, they concentrated on their Swabian estates for some decades as highly successful businessmen. There is no question of a continuous decline. Some successors made temporal and episcopal careers. Principally in the course of the Thirty Year War (1618–1648), the Fuggers withdrew increasingly from unreliable commercial dealing, to which numerous Augsburg business families had fallen victim since the 16th century. In 1647, the Maestrazgo lease agreement ended. In 1657, the traditional old Tyrolean mines went to the monarch. The Fugger Family continues to exist today, in the hereditary lines of the Counts Fugger-Kirchberg, the Princes Fugger von Glött and the Princes Fugger-Babenhausen.

The view was, and still is, drawn upwards. The Fugger chapel in St. Anna's church – a precious testament to the religious faith of the Augsburg family.

A landmark of Augsburg:
the Cathedral with its two
dominant towers.

THE CATHEDRAL DISTRICT

Augsburg's Cathedral District is a historic jewel of urban architecture. Its compact area brings together so many characteristic and endearing qualities of this old, traditional city on the Lech. This livable and historically important part of the city around the proud-standing Cathedral is valued by longstanding residents and Augsburg connoisseurs alike because it is so different from the nearby city centre, with its shopping streets and ubiquitous hustle and bustle.

The Cathedral District, dominated by its centuries-old ecclesiastical tradition as an episcopal seat and, maintaining a distance from the mundane, though not averting itself entirely, radiates a particular calm. The Hofgarten and Fronhof between the Cathedral and the buildings of the former prince-bishop's residence, currently the seat of the Bavarian Government of Swabia, offer stressed office workers, weary tourists, couples, and mothers with their offspring a refuge amongst historical landscape and an unparalleled architectural ensemble. Lingering here is a special privilege for native Augsburgers and visitors with inside knowledge.

The atmosphere in the streets and narrow alleyways, in the shadow of the mighty church, with its towers soaring over 60 metres into the sky is still to this day largely shaped by its function as the seat of the Bish-op of Augsburg. If you want to get to know the special quality of the city, be sure to spend a good deal of time in the Cathedral District, and particularly the edifice that has given the quarter its name. Natives and strangers alike strolling leisurely through the Cathedral District and open to the genus loci, the special mood of the place, will be richly rewarded time and again. They are accessing a small microcosm that brings to life the heritage of one of the oldest districts of Augsburg and its unique individuality.

The few broad streets, with their impressive houses, whose stately façades proclaim their self-confidence and their founders' sense of mission, the narrow, winding alleyways, in which first the clergy, subsequently artisans and Bavarian-Swabian tradesmen, found their homes, and, foremost, the church buildings and complexes, which keep their distance from the secular part of the city – all go to make up the architectural variety of the quarter. They invite you to roam hither and thither out of curiosity, and to absorb the particular charm of the place. If you reach the Cathedral by walking from Karolinenstraße via Hoher Weg, you already feel you have left the city behind when you have climbed to Obstmarkt and Schmiedberg. The impression is heightened if you take a few steps from Frauentorstraße into one of the many alleyways, their names telling of the vocations of their former residents: Pfaffengässchen, Karmelitengasse, Jesuitengasse.

This is where the Cathedral clergy took up residence when they began to give up their way of life in the monastery after the mid-11th century, and built the Domherrenhäuser, which was named after them. A typical example is Kustosgässchen 5, the fabric of which dates from the 16th century, or the former Domdekanei (cathedral deaconry) at Hoher Weg 22/24.

In the streets in the immediate vicinity of the Cathedral and Residenz, you are in the centre of the mediaeval episcopal city, the subsequent "cathedral city". Its oval shape, located at the south of the Roman city, can still be clearly seen by the courses of the streets in the city plan. The northern city wall, visible from Jesuitengasse, extends westwards and eastwards between Äußeres and Mittleres Pfaffengässchen and Frauentor, which was only demolished at the end of the 19th century. This is commemorated by a plaque at Frauentorstraße 7/9. To the west and south, the mediaeval city wall ran along the foundation wall of the old Roman wall at the row of houses at Im Thäle, Hafnerberg and Obstmarkt, via Mauerberg, where it was bordered by

the eastern slope of Lechtal. The city gate at the southern end of Hoher Weg was demolished in the late middle ages.

But we now turn our attention to the structure that gives its name to the district, not just because of its outstanding size and architectural majesty, but mainly due to its historical importance and allure.

A description claiming to even approximately cover all the attractions of the Augsburg Cathedral would fill several volumes. And so – in full awareness of the subjectivity of the choice – we first direct the visitor's attention to a few outstanding objects that, perhaps more than others, present a picture of the building, the district, the city and its rich history.

First, there is the church building itself, whose magnificent, richly ornamented south portal (ca. 1356) faces the civil Imperial City as a show façade. The cathedral, unlike the Church of St. Ulrich and

The 15th century cloisters are now reached via the Diocesan Museum (bottom). The interior of the Cathedral with a view of the magnificent east choir (right).

Afra – the famous and similarly important basilica at the opposite end of the Augsburg thoroughfare – was built within the former city walls of the former Roman provincial capital of Augusta Vindelicum. Experts consider this circumstance as unlikely to be derived from an early memorial to a martyr. Over the centuries, the Cathedral was expanded and reconstructed in many stages to become that which we see today.

With Bishop Simpert in the eighth century, we have the first reliable and historically watertight information about the building, which was consecrated in 805 or 807. Before that, a larger church building had probably stood there in pre-Carolingian times. The oldest part of the present cathedral is probably the crypt beneath the west choir, which was created in the 10th century. The Hungarian assaults towards the end of the first millennium AD inflicted serious damage on the structure. The famous Bishop Ulrich (probably 890–973), who was

so important both for the city and the history of the Holy Roman Emperor, had the Cathedral repaired again, fortified Augsburg with a ring wall and, by defending the city against the Hungarians, who were laying waste to Bavarian and Swabia, contributed to the momentous victory of King Otto I in the battle of Lechfeld (955). Otto I consequently became emperor. The defeated Hungarians for their part finally settled in the Pannonian lowlands and received the mission of the Roman Church.

A granite fountain in front of the Cathedral, with life-size bronze statues by the sculptor Josef Henselmann, has demonstrated Bishop Ulrich's importance for the Cathedral since 1986. The Bishop is shown on horseback, energetically urging the defenders forward, the cross in his raised right hand as a reminder of his role in the battle of Lechfeld. Next to him is the martyr Afra chained to a tree, the flames are already rising around her, in memory of her martyrdom. Beside these statues is Bishop Simpert, who is shown with a child and a wolf.

According to legend, the bishop rescued a small child from a rapacious wolf. If you visit the Augsburg Maximilian Museum, you will see many examples of this motif on old paintings. But the legend is

The numerous gravestones in the cloisters are graphic testaments to the faith of their age (left).
The former prince-episcopal residence with the Pfalzturm, now the seat of the Bavarian government of Swabia (bottom).

still alive: The Catholic Youth League of the Augsburg Diocesan Association has for some years presented the "Bishop Simpert Award" to young people for special services to children's welfare. But, against expectations, the bishop saints are interred not here in the Cathedral, but in the basilica of St. Ulrich and Afra.

The old bronze door of the Augsburg Cathedral, which is now kept in the nearby Diocesan Museum for conservation, where it is one of the museum's highlights, is one of twelve important Roman bronze portals in Europe and, besides the Cathedral in Hildesheim, one of the best examples of mediaeval metal casting north of the Alps. The large asymmetrical doors are ornamented with 35 cast bronze reliefs, whose meaning is difficult to discern because of missing parts. The most obvious interpretation is in the context of Christian symbolism: the church door as the boundary between the temporal world and divine paradise. The plates represent the battle between sin and redemption. The Augsburg bronze portal was created for the Ottonian cathedral consecrated in 1065. It was probably originally situated at the east side, since there was a large forecourt here. In 2000, the south side of the Cathedral was fitted with a new portal door instead of the Roman door. The sculptor Max Faller created it with 28 bronze reliefs of biblical subjects. The theme is God's creation, which is completed by the life-giving influence of the Holy Spirit. In its entirety, the relief is a pictorial bible in the tradition of the biblia pauperum.

In the interior of the church, visitors can find a wealth of artistic treasures. The cathedral holds a particular jewel of sacred architecture and stained glass in the west transept. The architectural composition, encompassing seven windows rows, represents the theological importance of Mary as the Throne of the true Solomon. The work of art takes up almost the entire southern wall of the transept. Because of the current position of the transept within the cathedral and its condition after several restorations, which made more or less sensitive interventions in the composition, it is not easy to identify the original important position attributed to the window by its creators. However, it has lost none of its splendour and narrative force to this day and captivates every attentive viewer.

The window mirror constructed on a pyramidal scheme is strictly symmetrical with respect to the centre of the seven window rows. The virtues Patientia, Iustitia, Temperantia, rising to the viewer's left and Bonitas, Castitias and Pietas to the right are aligned with respect to the representation of Mary with Child in the upper storey. A similar central position in the lower floor is taken by the Kings David, Solomon and Josiah enthroned there. This structure is flanked by various prophet figures. The comparatively monumental dimensions of the window and the complexity of the programme, which far surpasses any other iconographical examples of 14th century stained glass astonishes even aficionados and enthusiasts for this form of art. A remarkable feature is the repetition of the composition by the sculptures above the north portal, which were created approximately twenty years after the transept window.

Of similar importance and beauty are the five glass windows in the southern high wall of the nave. Here, the magnificently coloured prophets Jonah, Daniel, Hosea, David and Moses hang above our heads. They were probably created by an unknown artist around 1100 or in the 12th century, and are among the oldest known stained glass cycles in the world, which originally comprised 22 windows.

Another striking feature in the southern transept is the portrayal of St. Christopher on the west wall, which was created in the 15th century. The panel paintings by Hans Holbein the Elder, which ornament the four eastern pillars of the nave, also deserve the visitor's attention. The panels were probably originally provided as the wings of an altar for the monastery vineyard. They show the sacrifice of Joachim, the birth and presentation of Mary, and the Circumcision of Christ.

Not far from the cathedral is the former prince-episcopal residence. It is now the seat of the Bavarian government of Swabia. While all the other buildings of the former interior were rebuilt as unadorned official chambers, it has still been largely preserved in the east wing. In the west-east direction, it connects with the mediaeval Pfalzturm, the pivot of the entire complex. Within its walls, this wing accommodates the rococo festival hall, which is accessed via a magnificent fresco-decorated staircase. On its side walls are shown the three main rivers of the bishopric of Augsburg, by Johann Georg Bergmüller (1688–1762) – the Danube, Lech and Wertach. Between the windows is a medallion with the effigy of

The small Goldener Saal in Jesuitengasse with the ceiling fresco (1765) by Matthäus Günther.

the Roman Emperor Augustus. You pass via a small vestibule beneath the approximately 30-metre-high Pfalzturm, into the roughly 180 square-metre hall, which was clad with rococo wood carvings in 1752 by the artist Jakob Gerstens, who worked in Munich. The stucco ceiling with oil paintings showing the four continents was destroyed by bombs in the Second World War.

This festival hall was the site of the chapter house of the former bishops of Augsburg in the predecessor building. On June 25, 1530, the Confessio Augustana, the Augsburg confession of the Lutheran protestants, composed by Philipp Melanchthon, was read here before Emperor Charles V and the members of the Diet. For the 450th anniversary of the Confessio in 1980, a commemorative plaque was mounted on the outer wall of the Pfalz building, towards the Fronhof, below the Pfalzturm.

Experts don't regard the Augsburg bishop's residence as among the most important of baroque creations. But at the same time, it doesn't deserves any lower rank. As a historical and artistic monument it is a reminder of an abundance of historical events of European dimension and at the same time a symbol of the history of the city of Augsburg and the region of Swabia.

Those who prefer fresh air and nature will certainly enjoy the green spaces of the Cathedral District. It may be exaggerated to call the Fronhof a park, but its lawns and flowerbeds, its old trees before the backdrop of the Residence and Cathedral, limited by Peutingerstraße at the southern end, make it an impressive recreational area. Fronhof is named after the former episcopal court.

Towards the edge of Fronhof, south of the Cathedral, the Augsburgers erected the so-called "Roman wall" in 1954 and mounted numerous Roman inscriptions, sculptures and fragments on it. Besides architectural fragments and grave inscriptions, a Roman pillar tomb and a consecration inscription from around 215 BC deserve mention. In the mid-90s, they started to transfer the stone monuments to the Roman museum for better conservation, replacing the ones on the Roman wall with copies.

Another idyll in the Cathedral District should also be mentioned: the Hofgarten. It is among the favourite places of the Augsburgers, who are certainly not entirely unhappy that it is so well hidden, since they only have to share it with a few tourists, who usually find their way here more by luck than local knowledge. The Hofgarten, with its severely cropped box hedges and the symmetrical grounds, is still reminiscent of baroque landscape gardening. The ensemble of the five stone baroque gnomes, created around 1720, was certainly more extensive at one time. There must once have been twelve or more of the grotesque figures – as in other gnome gardens, such as Salzburg.

Also in the Cathedral District, can be found the Augsburg Mozart memorial in Mozart House at number 30, Frauentorstraße. Here, in an artisan's house, the composer Johann Georg Leopold Mozart, father of the far more famous son Wolfgang Amadeus Mozart, was born in 1719. It houses a standing exhibition of the life and work of Leopold Mozart and is the home of the German Mozart Association.

At the edge of the Cathedral District, a little hidden away in a niche in "Schwedenmauer", a connecting wall with stairs between the upper city fortifications at St. Stephan and the Unterer Graben (moat), is the statue of the "Stone Man" – a symbol of Augsburg. In the first half of the 19th century, a legend grew up that it was a portrait of the baker Konrad Hacker. Hacker, who wanted to rescue the city from the besieging Swedes during the Thirty Years War used the last flour to bake a loaf of bread and appeared with it on the city wall. He wanted to show the Swedes that Augsburg was not starving yet. But the besiegers shot the baker's arm to pieces, and he died shortly after.

The world-famous poet Bertolt Brecht, another son of the city, who walked past the "Stone Man" on his way to school, may have given it a new lease of life on the modern stage in the form of the mute Kattrin in his play "Mother Courage and her Children". Kattrin, who also rescued a city in a similar situation in the Thirty Years' War, is also shot dead. She had lost her voice after a childhood attack, and, in the introductory words to the play's climactic scene, it is said of her: "The stone begins to speak."

And how true that is! Augsburg's stones speak constantly. And not only the stones. The works of art, the gardens and grounds speak; the people, the museums and well-stocked libraries and collections, the specialties – all relate the life in this wonderful city through the centuries. You only have to learn their language and listen to them. The Cathedral District is an outstanding place to begin.

---

❶ **Cathedral.** It is possible to trace the history of the Cathedral back to the year 823. The oldest part is the crypt beneath the west choir started in the 10th century. There are frescoes from the Romanesque and Gothic periods, vault paintings and 4 panel paintings by Hans Holbein the Elder. The windows depicting the prophets Jonas, Daniel, Hosea and Moses are an example of the earliest stained-glass figures in Germany (middle of the 12th cent). The bronze door on the south side of the nave dates from around 1356 and comprises 35 relief panels featuring scenes from the Old Testament. In front of the Cathedral are the remainders of the Church of St. John (10th century) and relics of the Roman times.

❷ **Former Episcopal Residence at the Fronhof**
Built in 1743 in place of the Imperial Palace it retains one medieval tower heightened 1507/08. It was in the former chapter hall that the "Confessio Augustana" was proclaimed on 25 June 1530. Now it is the seat of the government of Swabia.

❸ **Courtyard**
Gardens, once part of the bishop's residence (approx. 1740), enlivened by rococo dwarfs, figurines and busts.

❹ **Little Golden Hall**
Jesuitengasse 12. Once an assembly hall of an early Jesuit College, with stucco by

Johann Michael Feichtmayr (1765) and a ceiling painting by Matthäus Günther. The Golden Hall is used now as a concert hall. Admission for functions only.

❺ **Peutinger House**
Peutingerstraße 11. Residence of the humanist and "town-clerk" Konrad Peutinger built in the 16th century with a delicate rococo facade which dates from 1763.

❻ **Churches of the Holy Cross**
The Catholic Church. This church, of a former Augustine canonical chapter dating back to 1195, was built in the Gothic style in the 15th and 16th centuries. The baroque work was created by J. Herkommer in 1719. After the destruction wrought by the war it was restored in 1949, in order to convey the unpretentious Late Gothic impression of space. Paintings by Rubens, Vermiglio and Kager. The Crucifix is the work of Georg Petel. The Protestant Church, a typical protestant church built between 1650–53 in place of the Ottmar Chapel. Paintings by Tintoretto and Schönfeld.

❼ **Burgkmair House**
Mauerberg 31. Once the residence of the Augsburg painter Hans Burgkmair. Early 16th century.

❽ **Gollwitzer Houses.** Volkhartstr. 10–16. In the years of rapid industrial expansions the architekt A. Gollwitzer erected these residential buildings in a "Moorish" style (1885–95).

❾ **Mozart House**
Frauentorstraße 30. A burgher house of the 16th–17th century. The house where Mozart's father, Leopold, was born is now the Mozart Memorial Museum. Open Wednesday through Sunday from 10 a.m. to 4 p.m.

❿ **Church of St. Gallus**
Gallusplatz. Today the church of the Russian-orthodox community. The core dates back to the 11th century. Renovated in 1589 it has a charming interior.

⓫ **Sweden Steps – Man of Stone**
15th century wall with steps leading from the higher ramparts near St. Stephan to the Lower Moat. In the lower part there is a 16th century Venetian wallfountain. In a niche of one of the towers there is a legendary figure of the Thirty Years' War known as the "Man of Stone".

⓬ **Bastion "Lueginsland"**
Part of the former town fortifications erected between 1430 and 1540.

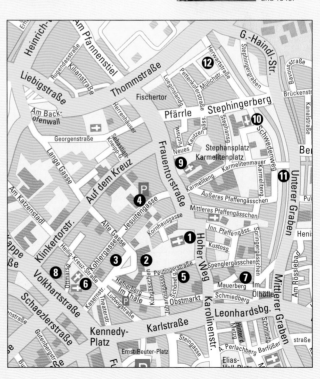

On the square in front of the Rathaus (Town Hall), schoolchildren gather in groups, enjoying the day. People run between them to catch the tram stopping in front of the Rathaus. The Stadtsparkasse bank on the corner is busy as customers withdraw cash for their shopping expeditions. The café tables beneath the sunshades are full now at midday with people meeting up with friends and colleagues. Tourists fold up their city maps and drink cappuccino. Augustus on his fountain, against the backdrop of the Neuer Bau, points southwards with a sovereign gesture, into Maximilianstraße, while below on the steps, one or other romantic sits reading a volume of poetry at the feet of the river gods. The multicoloured life of the city square is dominated by the Renaissance façade of Augsburg's Rathaus, and the elegance of the Perlachturm.

THE HEART OF THE CITY

Can any of those whose eyes are irresistibly drawn, time and again, by this world-famous ensemble imagine that the east side of Rathausplatz used to look entirely different? That four hundred years ago, people looked at a much smaller Rathaus, at a Gothic structure? That in earlier times there was no broad vista across the square, because, except for a small clearing for the Augustus fountain, it was all built up. Can today's sightseers be aware that what they see is just a snapshot; that the heart of the city is changing, and we with it.

Such changes may be the result of catastrophes, such as the night bombing of February 25 and 26, 1944, which levelled the buildings around the square to the ground, and reduced the Rathaus to just a soot-blackened façade. Or of civic resolve, which resulted in the Goldener Saal (Hall) of the Rathaus being restored to its former glory, faithful to the original. But the citizenry wanted to keep Rathausplatz itself ahistorically clear. Following an "open town-hall square" referendum, a construction trench that had already been

dug had to be filled in again. It is not inconsequential, what the heart of the city looks like, and how it changes. The impression that visitors takes home with them is shaped here; here, the identity forms by which the city community recognises itself. And those who have a chance to redesign the heart of the city are also designing the community's self-image.

If Augsburg is called a Renaissance city, that is thanks to Elias Holl, Augsburg's Municipal Master of Works, who gave Augsburg a new shape at the beginning of the 17th century. It was an urban reconstruction in grand style, which still shapes the modern image. Elias Holl took the city from a confined mediaeval town into the generosity and elegance of the Renaissance age. And the claim often heard in the city, that Augsburg is the northernmost city of Italy, probably has to do with the fact that Elias Holl gained inspiration for his buildings from a trip to Venice.

And how was it done in those days, at the beginning of the modern age, if someone wanted to replan a city and, above all, build a Rathaus that would exceed all conventions? First – much like today – they had to start from a favourable situation, and Elias Holl had that – the city rulers were amenable to his ideas; his urban reconstruction programme was in keeping with their ambitions. At the same time the city coffers were full to bursting and there was a body of craftsmen crying out for work. Thus, within a few years, the Municipal Master of Works had built more than a hundred structures, functional buildings, fortifications, but also many prestigious houses. The best known, and also to be admired today are the water and fortification towers, such as the Rotes Tor (Red Gate), then the Zeughaus (Arsenal), the Stadtmetzg (Slaughterhouse), Grammar School and Tower of St. Anna, the Neuer Bau on Rathausplatz, and the elevation of the Perlachturm (tower) into a campanile for the municipal bells.

But his chief work was the Rathaus, and, as Holl relates in his chronicle, a lunch with Remboldt, the Stadtpfleger of his day, proved very helpful in realising it. Holl used the opportunity to win the approval of the important municipal official for his plans to demolish the old town hall and, in its place, build a new, well-proportioned Rathaus. At the same time, Holl let slip that he "would very much like" to build it himself. The models of his plans can now be seen in Maximilian Museum. At the time, conservation of historic buildings was apparently not an issue. Today, decisions are not made nearly as easily, though a lunch with the right people at the right time is still a wise move.

Elias Holl's new Rathaus did actually become a magnificent structure, and so it still dominates Rathausplatz today – extremely idiosyncratic, with towers as majestic as they are original, and bearing no resemblance to any other building; a giant cube built on the slope; towering even more massively into the sky when seen from below – from Elias-Holl-Platz; one of the most important secular buildings of the European Renaissance; very elegant and full of confidence in the effect of its architectural clarity. Holl's Rathaus is still the political heart of the city. Here, the city council factions have their chambers; and the city committees meet here. However, the magnificent Goldener Saal is still reserved only for festive occasions. And the visitor, impressed by the extraordinary dimensions of the hall, and the portraits of emperors on its walls with their imperial authority, is astonished at the prestigious backdrop afforded by a free imperial city; a self confidence that continues outside in Rathausplatz, where, on the fountain over the city rivers, no one but the Emperor Augustus may stand.

Perhaps it was intended to accomplish something, this town hall, with its splendour, its iconography alluding to the Classical World, the emperor and empire, and the virtues of good government, beyond all ideologies. Perhaps it was intended to strengthen the urban community of the day, like an invocation of secular political authority in the face of the pent-up religious tensions that were latent in the city itself and throughout Europe, and were to break out in the Thirty Years War, even before Holl's Rathaus was completed. This war then spread to the city – with all its terrors, different occupying forces, plague and famine. Only a third of the population survived those dreadful years. Elias Holl, the great and highly praised Master of Works, who had rendered such great services to Augsburg, was ousted from office, since he was Protestant at the wrong time.

Like this early-modern opening up for the spirit of the Renaissance, the religious wars and conflicts about the true doctrine have shaped the heart of the city, and continue to do so to this day. Augsburg is a Lutheran city. Significant events of the Reformation and its reception have taken place in Augsburg, the scene of the great Diets as well as an Episcopal seat with an imposing cathedral. The famous interrogation of 1518, in which Luther refused to renounce his faith before Cardinal Cajetan, took place in the Fugger houses on Maximilianstraße. At the time, Martin Luther had lived for almost two weeks in the Carmelite monastery at St. Anna. In the same year, the Fugger chapel was consecrated in the west choir of the church, the first German Renaissance structure, the burial place of the Catholic Fuggers, who were resolute protectors of the old faith, not least because of their closeness to the Habsburgs.

Nowhere else can we feel the eventful and contradictory history of this age so intensively as in St. Anna. When the goldsmiths' chapel with its magnificent frescos was founded in 1420, the unity of the church was still unquestioned. In 1525, it was here in St. Anna that the Holy Communion was celebrated for the first time in Augsburg in "both forms" and the present church still breathes the spirit of the Reformation and is full of witnesses to these turbulent times. In the east choir, opposite the Catholic Fugger chapel, we can see the Reformer himself, painted by Lucas Cranach. The small museum of the "Luther steps" tells of the Confessio Augustana, which was read out at the Augsburg Diet of 1530 before Emperor Charles V in the chapter house of the Episcopal palace (now Fronhof), of the "Geharnischter Reichstag" of 1548, when the Emperor wanted to halt the progress of the Reformation by reference to his sovereign power, and of the Augsburg Peace of 1555 in the Rathaus – still the old Gothic one – which was also signed at a diet. This Peace guaranteed and protected the coexistence of the different confessions on equal terms by imperial law.

Whatever must have taken place on the Rathaus square in the age of the great diets!

At that time, this square was not only the centre of the city but the hub of the Empire. "Never, for as long as Augsburg has stood, have so many foreign people from so many nations come together," a contemporary said. The princes had journeyed with their delegations; the Kaiser himself stayed a whole year at the "Geharnischter Reichstag". Clerics and lawyers mixed with the royal household and mercenary soldiers, and the eyes of the entire empire were on this city, where world history was being written at the time. The unity of the empire was at stake, the power and influence of the princes and Fuggers, crises of faith and conscience, war and peace. And what was eventually decided affected the life of each individual citizen, craftsman and day labourer. "Cuius regio, eius religio," was the stipulation of the Augsburg Religious Peace; the sovereign ruled on religion in his territory. Those who didn't want to submit could leave. In the Free Imperial City of Augsburg, however, the citizen was able to choose between the two confessions.

But the Augsburg religious peace couldn't prevent the Thirty Years War, charged with religious conflict, from breaking out two generations later. But after that, parity in Augsburg was finally secured, equality of the confessions organised across all areas of the city. And parity also shaped the city, gave it an unmistakable form with the two twin churches St. Ulrich and the Heilig Kreuz (Holy Cross). Of the great festival with which the Protestants celebrated the return of their churches in 1650, no edifice has remained, but there is a holiday: the High Peace Festival on August 8, a special holiday just for the peace city Augsburg.

Today, this day is celebrated on the large Rathausplatz; where else? At the feet of Augustus with a view of the Perlach Tower and in sight of the Rathaus, which knows so much about the terrors of war; in the heart of this city shaped by religious conflicts, whose history tells so much about the necessity and the possibility of peaceful coexistence by people of different creeds and cultures. It is celebrated with a large festive banquet. Here, at this place replete with history, the entire multicultural city community sits down and eats together, once the peace messages of the religions have been read out.

The City Theatre, redesigned from 1952–1956. In front of it, on Kennedyplatz, the steel sculpture "Easter" by Matschinsky-Denninghoff.

On the right-hand side beside it, the neo-baroque State Library, built in 1892–1993.

Imposing houses of the late nineteenth century and chestnut trees in blossom give Konrad-Adenauer-Allee a special flair.

The quiet cloisters with the monuments of the affluent and benevolent citizens of the Free Imperial City of Augsburg.

West extension of the nave of the Protestant Lutheran parish church of St. Anna, with a view of the chapel founded in 1509 by Jakob Fugger.

Goldsmiths' chapel built on the north wall of the choir, with carefully restored late-Gothic frescos.

The religious peace of 1555 only applied to Catholics and Protestants. Today's "peace banquet" attracts a diversity of different faiths. Around thirty percent of city residents have a history of migration – reason enough to revise our view of the city in this respect, too. The Muslims with their different orientations and associations have set up a number of mosques and assembly halls, though they keep themselves to themselves. But there is a large synagogue in the city, built from 1914–1917 by the architect Landauer in the "Syrian" style, with a magnificent cupola and a generally very impressive complex on Halderstraße. The Jewish community was giving a very clear signal – we belong here; we are part of this city. Sadly, the fate of the Jews in Augsburg during the Nazi period was not different from other cities. The synagogue was desecrated, but fortunately not burnt down, so that it has been preserved and, since it was renovated in 1984, has once again given a home to a growing community. It is open to visitors and is impressive with its art nouveau splendour The Augsburg-Swabian Jewish cultural museum was created in the same building in 2006. It presents the history of the Jews as a part of the history of this city.

The synagogue on Halderstraße, which leads to the railway station, is no longer within the old city walls. From the mid-19th century, the Augsburgers felt too confined in the old fortification walls, which also no longer performed a function. The Free Imperial City had long been incorporated into the Kingdom of Bavaria and had become an engine of industrialisation. To create the necessary space, the city was rebuilt almost as comprehensively as in the age of Elias Holl. The fortifications were levelled at the western side, and the city opened up to the railway station, to symbolise its awakening into a new age. The Augsburg of the late nineteenth century developed along generously proportioned roads, stately houses for rich and influential citizens, who then, as the crowning glory of the newly created Fuggerstraße with its opulent houses, built a theatre in neorenaissance style, a symbol of middle-class civic culture and of a new self confidence. For this structure, they called on the architects Helmer and Fellner, who were very much in fashion at the time and had provided impressive temples of the Muses throughout Europe. The Theatre has since become the city's most important cultural establishment and is open to all. Indeed, whirling dervishes have even performed their ritual on its stage, announced by muezzin calls from the wings.

Near the theatre, another prominent cultural building arose at the end of the 19th century – the former City Library, now the State and City Library (Staats- und Stadtbibliothek). The contract for the project was awarded to the engineering company Maschinenfabrik Augsburg-Nürnberg, now known as MAN and one of the city's most important employers, because of its expertise with solid iron structures. With wise foresight, 166 metric tons of iron was used to make the building equal to the weight of all the books. The structure is strong enough to bear the roof extension that is currently planned for the growing library holdings. With its mediaeval manuscripts, graphic works and Mozart and Brecht collections, this house is a precious repository of the city's memory, and its holdings help us to comprehend the city as a distinctive identity even as its face changes constantly.

To return from the library back to the heart of the city, we can take the route through its belly, the city market. And that brings us back full into the present, the present of a vital, life-loving city that enjoys the feeling of well-being – history or no history. The city market is not only there for buying, but also a meeting point and information exchange. At the snack bar in the cheese hall, you can meet all kinds of people at midday from the offices round about; chat a while and smooth the progress of this project or that. You don't have to be agreeing on a new Rathaus. The goods are arranged in lanes and halls – vegetable lane, meat hall, fish lane and bread lane. The markets ranged around the Rathaus and along Maximilianstraße used to be specialised like that. Street names – Eiermarkt, Fischmarkt (egg market, fish market) – bear reminders of the times when the wares were not all concentrated in the city market. The abundance is overwhelming. The eye has already had its fill of the shiny aubergines and tomatoes, and bundles of herbs, long before they have been brought home and put in the pot. Here, cooks can find everything the heart desires – from selected fish and rare game to

The Jewish Synagogue in Augsburg, built from 1914–1917. Details of the magnificent "Syrian style" interior and dome.

Thora garment (Jewish Cultural Museum of Augsburg-Swabia).

the most unusual herbs and spices. The customers push and shove for exotic and organic produce, locally grown wares, but also imports from the other end of the world. The market is exceptionally colourful in the mornings, when the vegetable gardeners from round about are selling their home-grown produce and the multicoloured bunches of flowers from village gardens steal the limelight from the cucumbers and radishes. Here, beneath the tower of St. Anna, built by Elias Holl, we can vividly see and taste the diversity of cultures. Back to the Rathaus – only a few steps through the pedestrian precinct. At the end of a narrow passage, the square opens up to its full width, clear and unobstructed – except for the café furniture. To the left of the Augustus fountain, surrounded by children, behind it the campanile-elegance of the Perlachturm, then the Rathaus – always astonishing for its sheer size and originality. The towers at the corners, the quadratic force, the tower decorated with the imperial eagle and crowned by a cedar nut! The wide façade, planted on the square for all eternity. No. Even if rebuilding and replanning are part of the city's character – no one will dare to change anything here so quickly, not even after three lunches. Unless he's greater than Elias Holl…

⑬ Augustus Fountain

On the occasion of the 1600-year jubilee of the city in 1594 the Augustus Fountain was erected in honour of the Roman founders. Four figures on the fountain represent the water power of the city and present the rivers: the Lech with the rudder, the Wertach with gear wheel, the Singold with the horn of plenty and the Brunnenbach with the fischerman's net.

⑭ Town Hall

Built 1615-1620 by the town's architect Elias Holl, it is considered to be the most important secular Renaissance building north of the Alps. It is an expression of the self assertiveness of the former Free Imperial City. During the air-raids in 1944 it was burned down. After the war it was restored and in 1962 the interior was finished. For the town's 2000th jubilee in 1985, the Golden Hall, with its coffered ceiling and restored mural paintings was renovated. On view daily from 10 a.m – 6 p.m. (exept when closed for special functions) Information: Phone 3 24-91 80.

⑮ Perlach Tower

The Perlach Tower and the Town Hall are the landmarks of the city. The tower rises above the west choir of the collegiate church of St. Peter of Perlach, built in 1182 and altered in the 18th century. The base of the tower is 11th–12th century. The bell lantern and dome are the works of Elias Holl 1614. From its height of 70.4 meters one has a beautiful view. Open May through mid October from 10 a.m to 6 p.m.

⑯ Maximilian Museum

and Welser Gallery Philippine-Welser-Straße 24. An eaves-side burgher house of 1546. The paintings of the facade have been restored according to old pictures. Collections of town history, Augsburg arts and crafts are on display.

⑰ Fugger Statue

Provided by King Ludwig 1st of Bavaria in 1857 in honour of Hans Jakob Fugger who sold his valuabe library to the Bavarian duke for a very low price. This library supplied the basis for the Bavarian State Library in Munich.

⑱ Church of St. Anna

Established as monastery and church by the Carmelite monks in 1321, it was extended towards the latter part of the 15th century. The Goldsmiths' chapel (1420–1496, Gothic murals) was annexed. Converted to a Protestant church, the interior with the burial chapel of the Fuggers which is considered to be the earliest German Renaissance building. Some of the valuable paintings are by Lukas Cranach and Jörg Breu. The pulpit is by Heinrich Eichler and the tower by Elias Holl (1607). Luther steps: documents, pictures and tablets of the beginning of the Reformation in Augsburg. Closed on Mondays.

⑲ Municipal Theater

First built 1876–77 according to plans of the architects Fellner and Helmer. After the destruction caused by the war the Municipal Theatre was restored in a simpler style in 1956.

⑳ National and Municipal Library

Schaezlerstr. 25. The National and Municipal Library was built in 1892–1893 by Fritz Steinhäuser and Martin Dülfer. Architectonic sight from the turn of the century.

㉑ Prinzregenten Fountain

Prinzregentenplatz. The fountain with a statue of the Bavarian Prince Regent Luitpold was erected in 1903.

㉒ Main Railway Station

The oldest railway station concourse of a city still in use (1845). Enlarged 1869 by Friedr. Bürklein in the late classicist style.

㉓ Synagogue

Halderstraße 8. Built by F. Landauer and H. Lömpel between 1914–17, restored in 1984. The dome-shaped building has an art nouveau interior. Jewish Cultural Museum of Swabia-Augsburg: Religious and ritual objects. Tu–Fr 9–16, Sun 10–17.

㉔ Church St. George

Late Gothic church (1490–1505), with onion dome. Badly damaged in 1944.

㉕ Church of St. Jakob

The chancel dates back to 1355 and the nave was rebuilt in the 18th century.

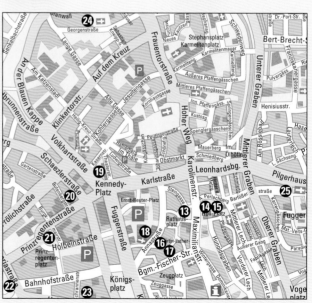

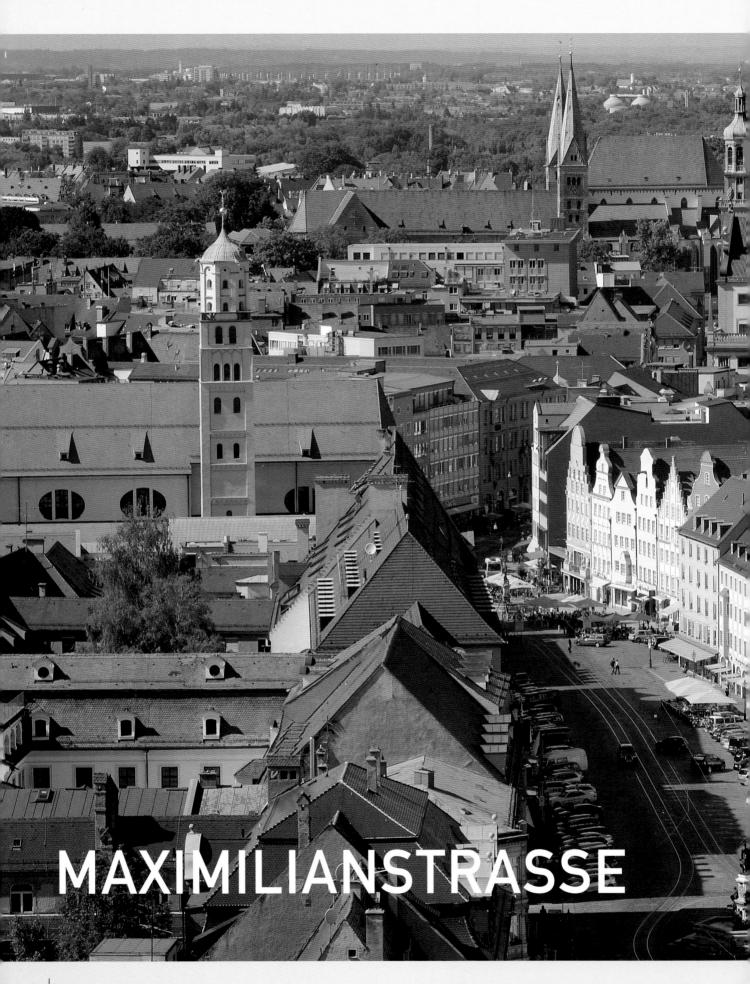

MAXIMILIANSTRASSE

For some, Maximilianstraße is the finest street in Southern Germany, for others, in the whole of Germany, and yet others consider Maximilianstraße the "finest Renaissance street in Europe". Whatever your emotional attitude to it, one thing is clear, in cultural history, it has a European dimension.

In discussions about Maximilianstraße, one question keeps coming up, namely how will we treat this glorious mile in future? How will we shape this history-laden street, between the Cathedral and the two St. Ulrich's churches? But before we examine that, I would like to go into the street's "European dimension". For me it is demonstrated by two components. The first is the historic events that have taken place along this glorious mile, and the second, its architectural jewels.

Come with me for a walk along the fascinating street. We start at the imposing basilica of St. Ulrich and Afra, which forms a worthy termination to Maximilianstraße at its southern end. The Catholic church, the second biggest sacred building in Augsburg, together with the much smaller Protestant church of St. Ulrich, demonstrate the religious parity in this city.

That was not always the case. The peaceful coexistence of religions only became possible with the Augsburg Religious Peace of 1555. This contract – concluded shortly after the Schmalkaldic War and the princes' rebellion – prevented over 60 further years of blood spilling. The peace treaty of 1648, the "Westphalian Peace", developed into the "Augsburg Parity" almost one hundred years later. As a consequence, all public offices of the Imperial City, from the city superintendent to the night watchman, had to be doubled up, or filled alternately in rotation, right up to the beginning of the 19th century. The principle of "double staffing" can also be seen in the Augsburg ecclesiastical landscape.

The "Confessio Augustana", ("Augsburg Confession"), should also be mentioned in this context. The proclamation of these Protestant demands before Emperor Charles V, at the Diet of 1530, can doubtless be seen as an event on a European scale. It took place at the northern end of Maximilianstraße, in the Cathedral quarter. A building inscription in Fronhof reminds us of the courageous stand by Melanchthon and the prince electors.

Back at the southern end of the street, we walk from the two St. Ulrich's churches into Ulrichsplatz, and from there to the west side. Here, after a few steps, we can see the house of the famous piano and organ builder, Johann Andreas Stein (Ulrichsplatz 10). Stein was a friend of the Mozarts; Wolfgang Amadé Mozart was rapturous about his instruments. In 1777, Stein was visited by Mozart with his mother and his beloved "Bäsle" (i.e. female cousin). This "Bäsle" was also the reason Mozart didn't just leave Augsburg the same year. Annoyed by a "Casino" that was very late coming into being, and the parsimonious behaviour of the Augsburg patrons towards a private academy in the Geschlechterstube, he wrote to his father in Salzburg: "I regret having journeyed here. I would have never believed in all my living days that, as Augsburg is still my Papa's home town, his son would be so affronted here." And, in the same letter, he continues: "I can say this, that if such a good [male] cousin and so dear a Bäsle were not here, I would regret as much as I have hairs on my head that I ever came to Augsburg.

The Mercury Fountain (top right) and the Hercules Fountain (bottom left), both designed by Adriaen de Vries.

Now I must write something about my dear Bäsle. But I will save it until tomorrow; one must be in a cheerful mood to praise her properly, as she deserves."

But his father was not so enthusiastic about this relationship and sensed that the flirtation would not have a happy ending. In his reply of October 12, 1777, he went into detail about the circumstances in Augsburg, writing: "It seems to me that she has too much familiarity with clerics. If I am deceived then I will apologise to her down on my knees through pure joy, since I only say: so it appears to me, and the appearance deceives, strangely so far – from Augsburg to Salzburg, strangely now that the mist is descending such that one cannot see 30 paces – now you can laugh as much as you want! It is all right that she is bad: but men of the cloth are often much worse." Though Wolfgang didn't want to accept it, his father's fears were justified. Maria Anna Thekla Mozart caused a full-blown family scandal in 1784 with an illegitimate child. The anonymous father was very probably an Augsburg canon. Opposite the Stein house is number 87 Maximilianstraße. This building, too, housed people who have had a lasting effect on history – in this case the life of the Empress Elisabeth of Austria. The daughter of Elisabeth's brother Duke Ludwig was born here. Marie Louise Elisabeth, later Countess of Larisch-Wallersee, was long Elisabeth's favourite niece. But then Rudolf, the only son of the Augsburg-native Empress Elisabeth, broke up with his sweetheart Mary Vetseras. Marie Louise Countess Larisch-Wallersee was thus partly responsible for the tragedy of Mayerling, at which Elisabeth's only son Rudolf committed suicide. She was therefore banned from court and went to America. Following an adventurous life, and completely impoverished, she returned to her home city and died here in 1940.

After this sad event, let us go on to a place where happiness dwelt. At least for one night – for the opening of the wonderful rococo hall in the Schaezler Palace on April 28, 1770, the then fifteen-year-old Marie Antoinette danced to the light of 365 candles. The bourgeois building owner, Benedikt Adam Liebert von Liebenhofen, was delighted by the eminent visit. His spending on the princely palace and the magnificent festivals – intended to mark the social climbing of the Augsburg banker and silver dealer – had brought him to the edge of ruin at various times. But then the daughter from a "good home" – her mother was no less a personage than Maria Theresia – was highly impressed by the ceremonial hall. Liebert had spent truly royal sums of money on it. The owner had commissioned artists of the first rank – the Munich Court Building Superintendent Carl Albrecht von Lespilliez as architect, Franz Xaver and Simpert Feichtmayer for the stucco, and the Roman Gregorio Guglielmo was responsible for the frescoes. The latter painted the ceiling of the ballroom with an allegory about worldwide commerce.

Commerce, more precisely money dealing, was also the stock in trade of the subsequent owner, who gave his name to the house. Dr. jur. Wolfgang Freiherr von Schaezler donated the Schaezler Palace to the city of Augsburg in 1960, on condition that this rococo jewel should be used as a museum. Now the palace contains the "Deutsche Baroque Gallery", the graphic collection with over fifty thousand prints, works from the Karl and Magdalene Haberstock foundation and the State Gallery of Old German Masters. These collections make a visit to the Schaezler Palace a must for every visitor to the city. For, who would want to miss a Peter Paul Rubens, Van Dyck or Tiepolo? In the State Gallery of Old German Masters next-door, you can find impressive works by Albrecht Dürer (if the Munich galleries haven't borrowed him yet again), Hans Holbein the Elder and Hans Burgkmair the Elder. And Doris Lieb must have been thinking of this impressive museum when, in her book "a walk through Augsburg" she wrote: "A door to world art opens here".

But now to the family that made Ausgburg the leading financial trading centre of Europe in the early modern age. The wealthy Fuggers also built their representative dwelling in this glorious mile. After the almost 40-year-old Jakob Fugger had married the 18-year-old Sybilla Arzt in 1498, the financial genius of the Renaissance needed a suitable place to stay. Jakob Fugger acquired several houses on the wine market and had them pulled down. In their stead, a new Fugger House was built between 1512 and 1515. It consisted of a princely hall, inner courtyards in Renaissance style, such as the impressive Damenhof, and grand room in which the emperors Maximilian I and Charles V, but also Titian or (as uninvited guest) the Swedish King Gustav II Adolf stayed. Martin Luther was interrogated here by Cardinal

Magnificent interior courtyards with round arcades and Tuscan pine columns in Italian Renaissance style. Damenhof (top) and Serenadenhof (right); interior courtyard of Höhmannhaus (left).

Cajetan in 1519 – he was required to deny his theses, which he famously did not do. He preferred to leave the city secretly and continued his criticism of the church and the Fuggers elsewhere – not least because of the selling of indulgences that they performed on behalf of the Pope. In 1777, Mozart played in the Fugger's concert hall. The 68-metre-long façade bore an impressive fresco showing scenes from the history of the Fuggers. This richly decorated, coloured façade of the Fuggers' city palace also fell victim to the bombs in the night of February 25 to 26, 1944. On this onslaught, after 200 American bombers had already attacked the Messerschmitt factories in the afternoon, British bomber squadrons flew two waves of assault. The 248 British bombers subjected the city to a 40-minute inferno, followed an hour later by 290 more British bombers. Irreplaceable cultural treasures were completely flattened.

The impressive Fugger Palace, a glorious mixture of High German City House and Italian Palace, was and, following its reconstruction, is once again a testament in bricks and mortar to the economic power of the Fuggers and the Free Imperial City of Augsburg. A demonstration of power and might can also be seen in the decorative fountains of Maximilianstraße. These fountains were created from 1588 to 1602, and, as works of art, must be described as of European ranking. The oldest of the fountains is the Augustus Fountain, created after models by the Netherlander Hubert Gerhart. The fountain statue on the pillar represents the roughly 50-year-old city founder Augustus posing as though addressing the army. Symbolic figures characterise the four river gods on the edge of the basin. The Lech with a pine cone, wolf skin and paddle; the Wertach with a crown of grain ears, and a quarter cogwheel as an allusion to the mills. The two smaller rivers, Singold and Brunnenbach, are given attributes such as a cornucopia and jug, and fishing net and oak-leaf wreathe.

The other two decorative fountains were designed by Adriaen de Vries and cast by Wolfgang Neidhart of Augsburg. The Mercury Fountain (created until 1599) with the classical patron god of merchants and tradesmen symbolises the rise of the city through the great merchant families. The Hercules Fountain (completed in 1602) is dedicated to crafts. It is intended to symbolise the controlling of water in Augsburg. The utilisation of water in the form of the Lech canals represents the rise of the guild, and is of great importance for the development of the city.

Adjacent to the Fugger houses, created in the 18th century as a "princely hostelry", the present-day Steigenberger-Drei-Mohren Hotel can look back at a long and noble past. The guest-books of the house are something special. The first high-ranking overnight guest entered here is the Prussian Soldier King Friedrich Wilhelm I, anno 1730, followed by Wolfgang Amadeus Mozart (1763 and 1766), Goethe (1790), Tsar Nikolaus I (1838) or Franklin D. Roosevelt (1905), who visited Augsburg on his honeymoon.

To complete our tour, I would of course like to recommend that you visit our new tourist information bureau. It can be found in the very attentively designed Antoniushof, the former Limbächerhaus (Maximilianstraße 57). The former patrician's palace still contains parts of the ground-floor vault and remains of frescoes preserved in the fine, renovated interior courtyard. The house was leased by the most influential businessman in Augsburg at the time. Peter von Argon (1413–1452) officiated eight times as bailiff; from 1428 he was the richest citizen in Augsburg. In his trading house and residence, he accommodated King Sigismund in 1431 and Emperor Friedrich III in 1442. Now the Regio Augsburg Tourismus GmbH also receives royal persons in this upmarket atmosphere – namely its customers: the guests from all over the world. They are all impressed by this historic street. As commendation, the street is also known as the "Imperial Mile".

But how will the "Imperial Mile" be shaped in future. Not only the Augsburgers have been deeply absorbed with this question for some years. One thing is certain, if is suitably upgraded it could provide an important stimulus to tourism. The competition "The Imperial Mile – replanning the Maximilianstraße in Augsburg", sponsored by the city, already contains certain interesting features that I would like to discuss in detail from the point of view of tourism. Over the years, it has emerged that one of the chief measures must be the planning and upgrading of Ulrichplatz. And rightly so. Imagine, on a pleasant summer evening, you are listening to works by our excellent Philharmonic Orchestra, and gazing at the illuminated St. Ulrich's church. The blue of the sky deepens presaging the end of

Reading matter and fashions under historical groin vaulting (top); the Kathanhaus, Kapuzinergasse 10 (bottom).

the twilight hour. Gradually, the moon grows in prominence and starts to dominate the scenery. Wonderful!

The "Imperial Mile" plan also provides for an improvement in gastronomic quality. Important steps in the right direction have already been made with the expansion of outdoor hospitality and the standardisation of street furniture. However, the mesh fences around the outdoor areas must be regarded as only a provisional measure. Even if the contemplated traffic calming measures are realised, the atmosphere of the outdoor gastronomy must better meet the high standards of the Imperial Mile. In my opinion, the modern world should also have a stronger presence in the Imperial Mile. But whatever happens, we must be clear that Maximilianstraße is Augsburg's "representative mile". There may therefore be only one guideline for this magnificent street – a top quality design in a European dimension.

26 Mercury Fountain
Erected in 1599 to the design of the Dutch artist Adriaen de Vries and cast by Wolfgang Neidhart, this bronze statue represents Mercury – messenger of the gods and symbol of trade – with a putto at his feet.

27 Weaver's Guild House
A reconstruction of the Weavers' Guild House which was torn down to enable a widening of the road in the late 19th century. The facade paintings of the fifties have used the motifs of the original Weavers' Hall depicting the history of the Weavers' Guild of Augsburg.

28 Armoury
A one-time armoury built in 1607 by Elias Holl, featuring a sumptuous frontage in the maneristic style by Joseph Heintz with the St. Michael's Group of Hans Reichle cast by Wolfgang Neidhart.

In 1806 the armoury became the property of the Kingdom of Bavaria but was bought back in 1895. Since its renovation, 1978–80, it has been an educational and Adult Education Centre, Town Cinema and alternating exhibitions in the Tuscan pillared hall.

29 Church of St. Moritz
The canonical chapter of St. Moritz was founded in 1021 by Bishop Bruno and is today a parish church. After having been destroyed during the war it was rebuilt between 1946–50 by Dominikus Böhm. Wooden figures by Georg Petel and Ehrgott Bernhard Bendl as well as paintings by Georg Bergmüller were saved of the former baroque interior.

30 Houses of Fugger
Maximilianstraße 36 and 38. The residence and house of business of Jakob Fugger comprised several buildings. There are charming inner courtyards with arcades in the Italian Renaissance style, the ladies' courtyard with marble pillars and murals by Jörg Breu the Elder. Destroyed during the war. Restored in 1951.

31 Herkules Fountain
Designed by the Dutchman Adriaen de Vries and cast by Wolfgang Neidhart of Augsburg it was erected in 1602. Largest of the three monumental fountains. Hercules is depicted fighting with the seven-headed Hydra. On an intermediate ledge there are three bathing naiads. The construction of the fountain symbolizes the town's Roman

origin, its world-wide commerce and its abundance of water.

32 Schaezler-Palace
Maximilianstraße 46. The rococo palace of the banker Liebert von Liebenhofen was built to the plans of Lespilliez (1765–1770). Considered to be the most impressive rococo building in Augsburg.

The rococo ballroom is resplendent with carvings, ornamental plaster work, wall mirrors and the ceiling fresco by Guglielmi. Today it houses the German Baroque Art Gallery and the State Art Gallery. Open Wednesday through Sunday from 10 a.m. to 4 p.m.

33 Kathan House
Kapuzinergasse 10. An example of typical Augsburg facade painting of the 18th century.

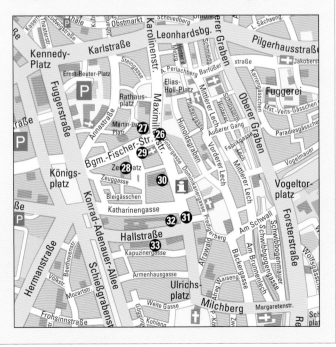

Closely packed together since mediaeval times, with a polymorphous roof landscape and prominent towers – the Ulrich district at the southern boundary of the Augsburg old town.

THE ULRICH DISTRICT

Oh, but it's high! If you walk through Peter-Kötzer-Gasse, from upper Augsburg down into Ulrich district and look around, your gaze is instinctively drawn upwards. High above the pedestrian rises the tower of St. Ulrich's basilica; So high that you feel small and insignificant beneath these massive buildings. The architecture of domination, you want to think, intended to make the power of the church and religion tangible.

Here, at the southern border of the old city, it is quasi at home, the Christian religion in Augsburg. This is where history left its first traces. From the sixth century, people revered a saint called Afra. She was supposed to have been a prostitute in the Roman city who converted to Christianity and was burnt for her religion. That is what the legend says. The Roman historian Venantius Fortunatus reported on the worship of Afra in 565. A Christian burial ground near the basilica became an early centre of pilgrimage; a first church erected over Afra's grave stood there; clerics and dignitaries were buried there in the 7th century. The Augsburg Bishop Ulrich also chose this place for his grave.

ANGELA BACHMAIR | 77

This Ulrich is better suited than Afra to give Augsburg an identity, especially since he is a real historical person. Born around 890 to a noble family, he must have been a cultured and courageous man, aware of his power. He extended the city fortifications built to protect Augsburg against the Hungarians, and he fought side by side with his knights against the Hungarian army in the legendary battle of Lechfeld of 955. After the victory, Ulrich helped King Otto to become emperor; Augsburg's importance for the Holy Roman Emperor was established and the episcopal city was able to unfold its economic power and glory.

Bishop Ulrich lived in his palace at the cathedral in the north of the early mediaeval city, but, at the southern end, he enlarged the church over Afra's grave and the monastery that had been there since the 8th century. After the turn of the millennium, it was occupied by Benedictine monks.

Little remains today of this monastery, which gave the entire district its name; as part of the diocese of Saints Ulrich and Afra

it was temporarily used as a royal Bavarian barracks after secularisation in 1803 and was destroyed by bombs in 1944. But the church of the diocese, which was elevated to an imperial diocese in 1643, still exists; the "basilica minor", as a Catholic city parish church is one of the most magnificent houses of God in Augsburg. Light-filled and high-vaulted, with carvings set in coloured and gold frames, huge altars and eight chapels, the church receives visitors with a calculatedly counterreformationist, quasi celestial radiance. The central group of sculptures on the high altar by Johann Degler and Elias Greither the Elder shows the birth of the Christ child together with angels and worshipping shepherds. Other altars tell of the Crucifixion (with bronze figures by the Schongau master Hans Reichle), the Resurrection and Pentecost, so that the church practically becomes a perennial stage for the church year.

With its high, elongated appearance, the Ulrich basilica forms the counterpart to the Cathedral at the north of the Augsburg old town, and at the same time the southern boundary of the thoroughfare through the

A glorious termination to Maximilianstraße, and symbol of Augsburg's religious parity: The Catholic St. Ulrich's Basilica and, in front of it, the Protestant St. Ulrich's church.

Imperial City, Maximilianstraße. But in front of the impressive silhouette of the basilica, there stands another church with the same name. The protestant St. Ulrich's church, which the Augsburgers also call "little Ulrich" was probably an antechamber of the monastery church at first, and was adapted for the Protestant service after the Reformation. With its modest size, the church identifies more with the residential houses round about than with the large basilica. The elaborately scrolled gable is reminiscent of the Protestant Heilig Kreuzkirche in the Cathedral district, similarly St. Ulrich's church, as a Protestant twin of a Catholic church, also alludes to religious parity, the equality of the two major Christian confessions. This was decided at the Diet of 1555 as the Augsburg Religious Peace to end a decades-long religious conflict (though it broke out again six decades later with the Thirty Years War).

But the Ulrich district doesn't just consist of churches. Less eminent people lived here – admittedly attracted by the monastery and its building activities: millers, bakers, weavers, smiths and butchers. They plied their trades beneath the large municipal markets along Maximilianstraße, in closely packed multi-storey houses with tiny shutters at ground level, with side aisles and small courtyards. Augsburg's social structure was also precisely differentiated along topographical lines – well-off tradesmen and patricians lived in the upper city, while the craftsman and small traders, the common people and have-nots, lived in the lower city.

Day labourers, too, were at home in the narrow apartment houses, occupied by many different tenants. The only light came through small windows or sometimes through the typical Augsburg low oriel; the workshops were often in the cellars. It must have been cramped and dark, in the narrow mediaeval alleys, which have been left so small after thorough but conscientious renovation of the quarter in the 1980s. The upper floor juts out, taking away even more light. Open galleries can still be seen here and there, with the timber framework, on which tanned leather or dyed lengths of cloth were hung out to dry.

Filled with light, with high Gothic vaults and later decorated in baroque splendour – the interior of the basilica named after the legendary Bishop Ulrich and the martyr Afra.

People lived here for centuries, in Zwerchgasse, Saurengreinswinkel and Kirchgasse, on Milchberg or Schwibbogen. The names take you back to the 14th century, when the Wagenhals suburb was incorporated into the city fortifications. The Wagenhals was the gallows ("Wag den Hals" – risk the neck); it was an area of low repute, whose buildings were simply torn down when they wanted to enlarge the city. With the extended city walls, one alley ("Gasse") was created crosswise ("zwerch"). Along the sloping road down from St. Ulrich, the council permitted milk to be sold – and the road became "Milchberg". Experts are still arguing about whether Saurengreinswinkel was called after an Augsburg citizen of that name, or because the ground here was poor – i.e. the "grit" was "sour". The building of residences in Ulrich district goes back even further: Augsburg's oldest preserved house, Am Eser 17, dates back to the 12th century. The soldiers guarding the Rotes Tor probably lived here. You can clearly imagine them keeping watch through the little hatch.

Located at the southern city boundary, Ulrich district remained clearly delimited by the city wall until well into the 19th century, and access was afforded by the Rotes Tor ("Red Gate" because of the colour of the tower) and the small Schwibbogen Tor (called after its arches). This little city gate ceased to exist in 1867, when the Augsburg city walls were levelled, but the Rotes Tor is still there: imposing, with bastion and bridge, wall and tower. Traffic to and from Italy passed through this southern city gate, and it was therefore of eminent importance for the city of Augsburg. In 1622, Augsburg's great city architect of the Renaissance, Elias Holl (1573–1646), designed the gate tower. It was the time of the Thirty Years War, and the Imperial City was investing in its military fortifications, and reinforcing the city walls and gates. Holl gave the tower rounded corners, supposed to deflect enemy bullets, and gave it a defensive appearance with light coloured pilasters and rusticated bands. He himself had not only defence in mind, but also an ornament for the city – he had "gracefully" plastered the tower, Holl wrote. In fact, the construction with the red and light-coloured stone alludes to the colours of the city coat of arms, and it is intended as a

city guardian, to command respect, and as an impressive reception building for outsiders.

At the point where the bridge of the bastion crosses the former city moat, there has been an open-air arena since 1929; smaller than the famous arena of Verona, of course, and less venerated with star performances, but nevertheless one of the first open-air theatres in Southern Germany. Italian operas used to be very popular at the summer festivals. Now a musical, opera or operetta is performed from the end of June to the end of July; always impressive against the spectacular backdrop of the city wall, Rotes Tor and water towers.

These three water towers – the large and small ones and the Kastenturm – tell a story of high-tech in the 16th and 17th centuries, of "Augsburg water technology" which was famed throughout Europe. Because Augsburg is higher than its two rivers, the Lech and Wertach, water lifting systems – fountain mechanisms that supplied the piped fountains of the upper city – were being built as early as the middle ages. The pumps of the 15th century main fountain machinery at the Rotes Tor forced the water into the high reservoir of the Rotes Tor. From there, it flowed into the city pipes – also supplying the series of decorative fountains along Maximilianstraße, dedicated to the strong Hercules, Mercury, messenger of the Gods, and the Roman Emperor Augustus as city founder. The master of fountains Caspar Walter (1701–1769) brought Augsburg's water technology to its zenith, and, in his day, the fountains of the Imperial City were a spectacle that was famed throughout Europe. Walter, the trained carpenter, also created the wonderfully carved double spiral stair case in the Kastenturm.

The official residence of the master of fountains was a house that – located beside the Lochbach – snuggles up to the water towers, so to speak. The "Haus bei den Fischen" ("House at the Fish") takes its name from the gargoyles next to the house door. The workshop and warehouse was the larger Brunnenmeisterhaus ("Master of Fountains House"), which is now to be found in the Schwäbisches Handwerkermuseum ("Swabian Muse-

Residents pick their culinary herbs from the herb garden at the Rotes Tor (top). The entire district – including Spitalgasse – has a human dimension.

Architectural jewels can be found at every step – along Schwibbogen-gasse, on Woll-markt and in Peter-Kötzer-Gasse.

um of Crafts"). Here, historic tools and workshop equipment, and samples of the diversity of historic crafts give a hint of how the residents of the Ulrich district earned their living before industrialization. The surgeon-barbers and dress trimmers, the beltmakers and cartwrights, the milliners and bookbinders. Bäckergasse ("bakers' alley") still reminds us of the historic handicrafts in the Ulrich district. Jewellery designers or picture frame makers, small galleries and artists' studios, fruit and vegetable dealers, bakers and butchers, the fashion boutique, the toyshop, the bicycle shop – small, distinctive shops that have not yet been dominated by the big chain stores.

Bäckergasse and its environs, with Kirchgasse, Waisengasse, Brunnenlech or Schwibbogengasse – has practically become Augsburg's alternative shopping area, appreciated by everyone looking for something special. And since, among the shops, there are also attractive cafés, bars and restaurants (but not so many that the normal residents have been driven out by the noise from the pubs at night), the Augsburgers very much appreciate the Ulrich district. In summer, you can sit with your cappuccino in front of the Annapam, Striese or Café Rufus and watch the schoolchildren going home, old people taking short strolls, or the glazier on the corner loading the vans with his fragile wares. This variety, together with the flair of the unspectacular, the completely normal and everyday, makes the Ulrich district so relaxed – it is a district where you can really live.

The quality of life in Ulrich district must also include its green spots. The city moat outside the former city walls, the wall gardens, have become the park of Ulrich district – with one of the many Augsburg Lech canals running through – lined with trees. A pleasant stroll takes you over bridges and steps up to the hill behind the Rotes Tor bastion. Alpine squills flower in spring, and the view over the treetops to the towers of the Rotes Tor, the waterworks and St. Ulrich's Basilica is perhaps one of the finest vistas that Augsburg can offer – an inner city idyll that you can only discover on foot, not by driving past. The city wall gardens are also the scene of jousting tournaments and historic games at the Bürgerfest every three years. Normally,

Of major significance for commerce and the transformation of the Free Imperial City was the Rotes Tor, which the architect Elias Holl surmounted with a fortified tower.

the fields belong to the children and young people for playing football, bathing (a large pool is filled in hot weather) and also for ice skating, when the meadows are flooded during a heavy frost in winter, and made into an ice rink. The Swabians are practically minded people, and also expect the green areas to provide some nourishment. That may be the reason why the city gardens department has created a small herb garden at the north of the city moat – on the model of a monastery garden, and therefore a reminder of the former St. Ulrich's monastery. Sage, pimpinelle, mint or basil can be picked here by anyone who needs herbs for their own kitchen. The free-for-all policy has worked for years without anyone plundering the gardens.

The people who live here seem to feel responsible for their quarter. For many years, they celebrated with a district festival in July. Washing lines were stretched across the narrow Kirchgasse and hung with pennants and all kinds of trimmings. The alley was filled with tables and benches; all of the residents brought some delicacies along, and guests came from all over the city, because they knew that Ulrich district was offering international specialties, exciting music and a good atmosphere. They chatted, danced, sang and drank until late into the night. From the 1960s, people from Italy, Spain and Turkey moved into the Augsburg old town (which hadn't been renovated then and offered cheap, though not so comfortable flats). The foreign workers brought a lot of children and a little Mediterranean flair into the Swabian city – mothers sometimes sat outside on chairs, watching their children playing; men strolled around chatting in twos or threes.

A lot has been done for old people here in past years, with the extension and modernisation of the St. Margareth retirement home and sheltered accommodation in the Heilig-Geist-Spital. That is the result of the demographic change, but also has a long tradition in Ulrich district. Not far from the Rotes Tor, the city had the Heilig-Geist-Spital rebuilt between 1625 and 1631 by its city architect Elias Holl. The home for the old, weak and sick had long run the alms office; now Holl was to build a house for 340 people in place

The Open Air
Stage, together
with the Augs-
burger Puppen-
kiste and the
historic water
towers form
part of the
Culture Park at
the Rotes Tor.

of the small and worn out old building. Alongside quarantine houses and almshouses or the pilgrims house further to the north, the Spital was part of the social infrastructure in the Free Imperial City. The "crazy" and ill came, but old people came to spend their twilight years here. Holl built the new Spital in a highly modern style for those days, with a bathroom and hospital, ovens, toilets and a washroom, as well as a mortuary and chapel. The architect designed his last building as a forceful four-winged complex with a yard surrounded by four columnar arcades and several storeys, as well as a hall with nave and aisles on the west side.

The front façade on Spitalgasse is decorated by a portal with volutes and entablature, but otherwise there is not too much ornamentation. Nevertheless, the Heilig-Geist-Spital is an extremely imposing structure, a regular architectural landmark at the southern edge of the old town. The 13 window axes of the west façade, the huge steep roof surface with its dormers to some extent dominate the small residences, and provide an optical counterweight to the large St. Ulrich's Basilica.

In the upper floors of the Spital, sheltered accommodation apartments were established in past years, connected via a glass bridge to the modernized St. Margareth's old person's home. This house is, so to speak, a legacy of St. Margareth's convent, and that brings us back to the church as the cornerstone of the Ulrich district. In the 13th century, the Dominican convent of St. Margareth was founded in the east of the Ulrich parish; three hundred years later, because the monastery produced too little income itself, it was added onto the Heilig-Geist-Spital. The richly decorated church, baroquised in the 18th century, forms, with its hexagonal tower, an impressive landmark at the corner of Spitalgasse/Margarethenstraße, and is still a Catholic hospital church.

But Christianity is not the only religion to have left its mark in Ulrich district. Next to Heilig-Geist-Spital is the address "Beim Rabenbad". But this wasn't a bath for Ravens, the name is said to come from a bathhouse built in 1290 for the Augsburg Jewish community. It became called the "rabbis' bath" and, after the expulsion of the Jews from the Imperial City in the 15th century, gradually became corrupted to "Rabenbad" (ravens' bath) – an interesting example of how language erases memory.

But not yet expunged from the memory of the residents of the Ulrich district are the people who lived in the – now closed down – municipal shelter for the homeless at

Rabenbad. They belonged to the district just as much as the established citizens or artists, and the landlord of the "Schwarzes Ross" opposite and the fruit vendor on the corner ensured that this place that what was actually considered a deprived area could be thoroughly integrated into the quarter.

Now, around Heilig-Geist-Spital, culture takes centre stage. The water towers and wall gardens are to be made into a "Rotes Tor culture park", with the towers as an accessible monument to the water technology, and the gardens as an experience zone, with many possibilities, from strolling to outdoor concerts. And the Spital itself houses Augsburg's best known cultural institution, the Augsburger Puppenkiste, the marionette theatre founded by Walter Oehmichen, who is associated with the name Augsburg throughout Germany. Jim Knopf and Lukas the train driver, Urmel from the Ice and the Little King Kalle Wirsch, Mikesch the Cat and the Sams with Mr. Taschenbier are at home here. All year round, the stars on strings attract children with their parents or grandparents to the stylish theatre, which was built in the former Spital sickbay, the hall with nave and aisles on Spitalgasse. Tickets are difficult to come by, even for the Puppenkiste's cabaret performances, at which Angela Merkel, Edmund Stoiber and other personalities from politics or economics, in the form of carved figures, entertain adult spectators.

The Heilig-Geist-Spital has become a regular tourist attraction, since the famous wooden puppets can be visited between performances – in the "Kiste", the adjoining puppet theatre museum. This fun marionette world gives a light touch to the Ulrich district – an attractive counterweight to the defensiveness of the walls and gatehouses, the dignity of the churches.

③④ St. Margareth and Wool Market

Church of a former Dominican convent dating back to 1594 and altered to the baroque style in 1720. Located to the east is the courtyard (16th century) and open pergola (Wool Market).

③⑤ Heilig-Geist-Spital with Brunnenmeister House and Water Towers

The Hospice of the Holy Spirit 1623–31 was Elias Holl's last work. A grand inner courtyard with arcades leads to the restored house of the Master of the Wells and Fountains and to the three water towers (16th–17th century). Now a Crafts Museum and Gallery.

③⑥ Freilichtbühne, Little Herb Garden

A little herb garden was planted in the northern part of the moat. This open-air theatre is to be found in the western moat of the Red Gate with the old fortifications in the background. Opened in 1929.

Performances are held every June and July (Opera and operetta).

③⑦ Rotes Tor with Bastion

This was the most important gate of the Free Imperial City through which the road to Italy led. The forward gate dates back to 1546. The gate tower was altered by Elias Holl. The earthwork of the bastion was raised in 1611 and is now a park.

③⑧ St. Ulrich and Afra

The construction of the abbey church of the Benedictine Monastery, self-governing under the emperor, was started in 1474. The chancel and its three massive altars were finished in the 16th–17th century. This Late Gothic Basilica with its 93 meter-high onion-domed tower is richly appointed in the Renaissance and baroque style with wrought iron grilles and numerous works of art. Tombs of the diocesan saints Afra, Ulrich und Simpert.

Evangelische Ulrichskirche

A former preachers' hall of the monastery, it became a Protestant parish church in 1524. In 1709–1710 it was rebuilt in the baroque style. It has a richly ornamented pulpit, a stuccoed ceiling and valuable paintings.

③⑨ The Swabian Crafts and Guilds Museum

in the former fountain keeper's house. The Swabian Crafts and Guilds Museum in the former fountain keeper's house offers a comprehensive overview of about 40 craft professions and their historical development. A unique collection of exhibition pieces allows the visitor to form a living picture of the traditional craft professions, Phone 32 59 - 2 70, Open: Mon–Fri 1 p.m.–5 p.m., Mon, Tues 9 a.m–12 a.m, Sundays and public holidays 10 a.m–5 p.m. By prior arrangement Tours possible, free of charge.

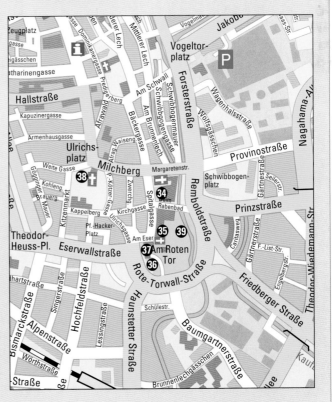

LIFE IN THE LECH DISTRICT

It's a privilege every day, for me. I look westwards through the window of my study at the finest ginkgo tree in the city. The ginkgo comes from distant China, and once again demonstrates how multicultural our Lech district is here. Throughout the summer, its luxuriant fan-like foliage gives a little verdancy to my view of the *Alte Silberschmiede,* then it turns pure gold in autumn, and suddenly, within a night, sheds all its leaves onto Pfladergasse and the small courtyard of the Pfladermühle. Mothers with prams fill carrier bags with the golden foliage. An elderly gentlemen coming from the nearby antique shop also stoops to pick up such beautiful bookmarks.

In front of the east windows of my apartment, the saddest weeping willow of the city lets its weeping branches hang to the floor and over the rushing canal water. Why should it be so sad? Alas, there are some architectural offences, omissions in the old city – otherwise so perfectly renovated. Perhaps the old willow is sad at the litter that is often carelessly thrown into the Vorderer Lech, and clogs the mill weir around the corner. Perhaps it is also sad at the sorrowful state of the Gignoux House further up. A rococo pearl, in which the *Komödie,* the playhouse of the city theatre, has been leading a provisional life for ever. Indeed, that is where I acted in the theatre for the first time in Augsburg. A few years ago, I was allowed to perform there, and noticed that almost nothing in the building had changed since my youth. At that time the canals south of the city, which were probably branched off from the Lech in Roman times, were almost entirely covered up and out of sight, but a premium residence for rats and cockroaches. Since then, the fast-flowing Lech brooks have been opened up almost everywhere, provided with decorative wrought iron railings and many small bridges, and, in the

The "Kresslesmühle" tempts you with jazz, Finnish coffee, cabaret days and programmes for children of immigrants.

summer heat, provide refreshing cool in the narrow alleys. Augsburg is supposed to have more bridges than Venice, though I consider that just a rumour – they count every plank gangway to the house entrances. The canals used to be the vital energy arteries for the countless craftsmen's shops, their smithing hammers, grinding, drilling or polishing machines driven by the primal force tapped from the wild Lech. The tanners and papermakers also used lots of fresh water.

The house where Brecht was born, *Auf dem Rain 7,* was also located next to the canal; now a memorial to the great poet, the iron hammers of a file factory struck their harsh rhythm when he was a baby. That may be one of the reasons why the Brecht family moved to the quieter pastures of a MAN works apartment by the silent *Kahnfahrt* (boating lake). The Lech district, now my area as well, was the territory of the young Brecht and his schoolfriends, with their local pub, the *Gablers Taverne,* narrow alleyways with secluded spots for young lovers, and wild songs to the sound of Brecht's guitar. My address is *Beim Märzenbad;* this may have been a horse watering place at one time, where the nags of the Imperial City were watered, and later became a bathhouse of a certain Mr. März. I don't need to imagine that a barber's daughter called Agnes Bernauer once lived here. But the idea of a horse watering place is more romantic than modern car washes at any rate.

I decide to take an afternoon stroll, so that I don't leave anything important out of my account. Hence, from the cool house entrance I walk beneath the weeping willow, then turn right over the wide paved bridge, and follow the canal. On the left is the new annex of the nuns of St. Margareth, with a sloping glass walkway from the old building to the new. Above, the sisters have had an attractive roof gallery built, where they grow flowers and can enjoy the sun. The house next door is also over 400 years old, and on the ground floor has a rare groin brick vaulting, an uncle of the famous city architect Elias Holl is said to have built it.

Opposite is a semi-renovated semi-ruin. Holding onto the iron railing by the stream, a young couple perform veritable Qigong exercises, smiling and completely self-absorbed. The pretty young woman appears to be Asian; no one can say that we're not global multiculturals here. And I've already reached the Wirtshaus *Zum Bauerntanz*, an ancient pub with a few outdoor tables. In my early years in the theatre, this was an establishment of Breughelian coarseness; now the restaurant has long been modernised on the interior, as has the preparation of the coarse traditional Swabian cuisine, which the city guides like to tempt their groups of visitors with. But on summer days, you can still enjoy beer and a very high calorie snack in the fresh air. And people of every colour and profession look on. If I strike lucky, as recently, the jazz musician Wolfgang Lackerschmid, who is famous in the city and worldwide and runs his *Traumraum* studio in the quarter, stops for a chat as he pushes his youngest by in the pram, or Eva-Maria Keller, one of the stalwart actresses of the local stage waves a greeting on her way up to the city theatre. A band of tourists is just entering the Bauerntanz. You can hardly get past them. People in groups show excessive self confidence. The city guide heads for the reserved seats inside, and then relates the story of how Italian cannelloni became Swabian Maultaschen. Of course, we've long been multiculturals here …

Just ahead, *Judenberg* rises to Moritzplatz and the upper city, framed by the colourful bunches of small flower shops, whose gentle fragrance is having an unfair fight with the more pungent odours from a kebab shop. Norbert is one of the florists and regularly wins window-display competitions. For Mozart year, a complete score has been enlarged to poster format; hundreds of musical notes written by hand. Pottery on the ground and sidewalk forces the eyes and feet to pay attention, especially since a biker is recklessly thundering down Judenberg. Keeping your eyes open is the first rule for appreciating the old city. That is the only way to be sure of not missing anything new and worthwhile.

Pfladergasse is probably our most typical alley in the quarter. The close-packed, narrow houses tower upwards. The former craftsmen's rooms have been partly rebuilt into original mini-shops – real antiques can be found here together with worn-out books, bric à brac, hand-knitted alpaca, Third World dolls, a real vinotheque, select handbags as art objects, rare jewellery. A tiny hairdresser's shop is jammed between the neighbouring houses, two Figaros snip and cut next to the open glass door, and there is the *Alte Silberschmiede* again: with a branch outlet especially for wedding rings – *die Eheringschmiede*. During Advent, they play music energetically in the courtyard almost every day, and I sit upstairs in the warm room behind my window, listening for free.

At last, I greet my ginkgo tree from the other side and arrive at Elias-Holl Platz. The majestic rear façade of the Rathaus towers grandly into the sky. At the left, a welcoming high-gabled row of houses terminates the attractive open space; there is a gourmet restaurant, the *Ecke-Stube*. It is part of the *"Die Ecke"* (the corner) artists' community, now a century old and also running a gallery for contemporary artists in one of the gabled houses. At the gallerist, Gottfried, an Upper-Bavarian, architect and brilliant figure drawer, I received a good espresso in the first floor and information about the new events in his second gallery, a well-equipped wine bar on Schlossermauer. Here, he has lovingly and expensively developed an old hostelry into a gallery and residence; he has kept the stone horse troughs and rings for tying up the animals in the wall on the ground floor. The houses there, on Schlossermauer, only 5 minutes' walk from here, the rear wall of the wide traffic route Oberer Graben, practically form the eastern boundary of the Lech quarter. I digress. But isn't it the best thing about living in the old town, to be able to wander about? Goals are found walking; there are always new discoveries to make, even if only a new view of a well-known alleyway. But now I'm here, at Elias-Holl-Platz, about two hundred paces from home. Another 35 double paces, past my master hairdresser *Matteo*, and I'm standing in front of *Kresslesmühle* – a menu on the terrace table tempts me with Finnish cuisine. The 'Mühle' (mill) is squeezed between the Vorderer and Hinterer Lech, and used to be called "Klessingesmul", whatever that may mean, it isn't Finnish. It used to be a grain mill and is now a cultural centre and meeting point; one of the main aims of the organizers is to integrate immi-

In Augsburg, there are supposed to be more bridges spanning the canals than in Venice.

Top right: The first district of the great Bert Brecht.

Below: Almost an insider tip, the "Barfüßercafé".

The spruced up "Alte Silberschmiede", at the right in the picture 'my ginkgo'.

grant children. And Thespian art on a small scale. Its enterprising head, Hansi Ruile, has created a good name for it in the German cabaret scene. On the annual cabaret days, everyone from the scene guests here in the large hall. But even (still) unknown native talents receive a platform in the narrow and winding theatre room. Jazz musicians are also welcome here. Hansi also managed the street festival *La Piazza* for many years. There were circus tents, variety booths or simple stages on every square and open space in our quarter; musicians, clowns, mime acts and performance artists, artistes of all kinds, showed their talents, there was grilled Armenian food and African clothing, and the old city was bursting at the seams with people. Even the people from the University came in hordes, it was really fine, and of course extremely multicultural. For inexplicable reasons, the city authorities allowed this superb festival to die out. I remember all this while I drink a fruit juice in front of the "Mühle", and look at the old *Stadtmetzg* (city slaughterhouse) opposite, another architectural work by the great Elias Holl. Now four stone ox skulls at the portals remind us of the buildings earlier purpose. The Vorderer Lech rushes, by after it has passed beneath Perlachberg, and then run direct and open through the slaughterhouse, where it used to provide cooling and carry away the waste from the carcases. Now, we read succinctly, the proud Renaissance building houses several city offices. My view of the Perlach tower is obstructed by the Fountain of St. George the dragon slayer. The bronze statue on it, a copy of the original, which has already stood at several places in the city, is only gradually acquiring a patina. The four gargoyles on the fountain pillar are supposed to have been copied from decision-makers of the day; they look much older than the Saint himself. Behind him rises the Perlachberg; at half-height is the *Café Euringer,* said to be the best address for cakes in the city. At any rate, they bake a renowned thin *Bienenstich* (honey cake) there. From the pinnacle of the Perlachturm, the heathen goddess Cisa flashes down as a golden weather vane; there is still a place for something heathen between the Cathedral and St. Ulrich.

Now I'm sitting down again because I wanted to memorize the details of this little tour of the quarter. I count my paces again to give the reader so inclined a picture of how close at hand everything is for us people of the Lech quarter; so just around the corner after 35 double paces I can enter the *Barfüßerkirche*. In the anteroom of the church, I discover a photo of Brecht; who would have thought it! I've just walked past too often. A high, slender, almost unornamented brick nave. It was largely destroyed in the war, and rebuilt in a very severe, sparse, pietistically pure way. Franciscan poverty and humility now characterise the peaceful house of God on one of the busiest arterial roads. Only a bulky baroque wrought iron screen separates off the altar. How pleasant that a tiny Café *Zu den Barfüßern* has been incorporated into the block and almost hidden away directly towards the open canal. Next to its entrance, Iwan runs his exclusive flower shop, with decorative specialities, from the rubber-tyre flower trough to the fallow deer surroyal. Of course, he also has some very nice flowers.

Diagonally opposite is the way to the Brecht house. 35 double paces, but then I have very short legs. During my youth in the theatre, there was still a strong dispute in the city about whether this "dreadful Communist pawn" should be performed at all. My colleague Gregor had just received an engagement after studying in Rome, and hit the nail on the head: "In Rome, they've just dedicated a university chair to Brecht, are you mad here…?" Fortunately, the attitude to Brecht has changed. The Bertolt Brecht house presents the information aesthetically.

And there are various Brecht festivities through the year. Just opposite the memorial, a bookbinder has lodged. The two ladies there know their trade. Brecht loved such things. Just a few paces more – counting the steps is starting get silly – I cross the wide Leonhardsberg and end up, like my underground companion, the Lech canal, at the Altes Stadtbad (municipal baths). This former art nouveau jewel was renovated and reopened just a few years ago. If I walk briskly and change quickly, I can be from my flat into the heated swimming pool within five minutes – if that isn't luxury? On the bridge next to the municipal baths, two youths are swigging bottled beer from the filling station, while vigorously exchanging opinions. A few houses further up is where I lived thirty years ago. Am Schmiedberg. At ground level is the pub *Zum Grünen Baum*. I lived in the upper storey with a few colleagues from the theatre. My room even had a charming old oriel. The landlord, host and cook was also a magician. He kept his guests amused for hours with conjuring tricks. As a cook, he was less successful.

All the way up to my room beneath the roof, the staircase smelt of repeatedly reused pork fat. And the toilet cubicles were also in the staircase... Now, a small, refined Italian has the say (and does the cooking) in the house. We are just so multicultural ... I take the return journey along the Oberer Graben, with a view of the rear façades of the tiny houses that must have clung to the reverse side of the city walls at one time. At Zigarrenhaus Mozart – that has nothing to do with the composer of the same name, and there aren't any cigars there any more, either – I slip back into the old city. The narrow alleyways, always accompanied by one of the Lech streams, with unexpected views into courtyards or gardens, stick together to form a real small-town idyll. Now I'm at the *Lustküche,* a small gourmet restaurant with open-air terrace. A young team headed by Chris, the also young chef, cooks superbly here – light, Mediterranean, also South German, but always imaginative, fresh and skilful. And inexpensive. Almost an insider tip. Estimated at about 70 double paces from my door.

At Holbeinplatz – the modern Galerie des Kunstvereins can be found in the house of the same name – I turn southward, the same ways as the canals, that is to say I go with the flow. I regret that I don't know, cannot measure how fast the Lech streams rush through our quarter. At any rate, I couldn't keep up with them on foot. On the left, an old tannery rises up. Animal skins used to be dried on the airy, open roof galleries.

Of the many tanners, only one is left: that of the *Aigner family.* They still tan naturally in the old way. And stitch leather goods. Chamois leather and suedes of all kind are the specialties of the house. Opposite is the *Reste Maier,* the Eldorado of tailors. But also

the costumier of my theatre days. Here you can find everything for sewing, lining, padding, and inexpensive. Around the corner, a wrought metalworker shows his grilles, fences, doors and gates. However, the artworks are created in the workshop far away in Lechhausen. It used to be different, when more silversmiths worked here than in any other South German city. Augsburg silver was sought-after at all the electoral courts and in all the major churches of Europe. Now it can be found in the great museums of the world. If only I could be transported back to those glorious days for just one day and then make a round trip like today.

There are a lot of bicycles chained to the bankside railings next to *"Thing";* the student pub runs a large, cool beergarden watched over by a mighty totem pole, multiculturals are everywhere. I walk as far as Am Schwall, to the canal that flows here from the gardens around Rotes Tor near the open air stage. Turning left, I soon come across the convent of St. Ursula, which runs a large girls' school. The girls in groups force the cars to drive at walking pace; quite rightly so. And then I'm back at Holbeinplatz; everything is nearby here; the quarter is handy, so to speak. A city water tanker fills the large plant tubs on the quiet square. I squat on a stone bench and take stock – is there anything I haven't mentioned in my account, anything I've forgotten? There's a lot I haven't mentioned about by favourite city quarter, that every visitor should discover anew for himself. Insider tips? Perhaps enumerate them according to the five senses? Sight? It's a good thing to keep your eyes open all the time here, day and night! I just found a leaflet in the bakery on Judenberg announcing a number of light installations along our canals for the following weekend, for the *"Long Night of Water".* Luxury right on my doorstep. There will even be a concert beneath my weeping willow. I can't wait. I've just thought of another luxury gift that the city occasionally offers – when there's an evening event in the Goldener Saal of the Rathaus and you walk across the square of the great Elias Holl at night, a coloured golden light shines through the panes onto the night walkers below. Of course, something so bewitching escapes the mass of tourists. Or if, as recently, roaming along *Hunolds-*

Paying attention is the first rule of enjoying the old city. That is the only way not to miss anything new and worth discovering.

Eisenberg leads from the Lechviertel past the town hall into the upper city, the draughtiest steps in town.

graben, I suddenly have to stand still because velvety saxophone tones drift from a garden, and I know that my friend, the wonderful jazz musician Stefan Holstein, is practicing in his garden for the next concert. Then I have a pure treat for my ears. I've already spoken a lot about the joys for the sense of taste. Aromas are surely the speciality of the herbs and spices shop at the end of *Bauerntanzgäßchen*. Ingredients from all over the world over the fresh smell of the Lech water shooting past. Sculptures that can be haptically experienced in the garden of Holbein House will satisfy the sense of touch. Next door, a small but fine chocolatiere recently opened, called, which I find witty, *Bitter-Sweet*. Just as Brecht affectionately called his first great love, Paula Banholzer. The charming chocolateuse maintains that she didn't know about the second meaning when she chose the name. But it fits in perfectly with BB's former territory.

My route home takes me past the *"Xangs-studio"* of Katja Kessler, and I remember that one of her best singing students is blind, and I see the young man before me, when, groping for orientation in wide semicircles over the pavement, he finds his way with swift and sure steps through the old city up to the music school (unfortunately it no longer exists). At the *Bauerntanz* ahead, two men in white coats sit in the windows and, almost in reverie, paint two old pub windows. There has always been life here, for centuries the everyday of the countless workmen and their helpers; their customers pushed through the alleys; more people were there then than push through here on their way from the City Galerie on a shopping Saturday.

Now the people are an out-and-out mixture, simply multicultural. Individualists. Each in his own way.

---

40 Stadtmetzg

This former Guild House and central market of the butchers was erected 1606—09 by Elias Holl to the for that time most modern standards. Two subterranean Lech canals were used for the cooling system and for the disposal of waste. Today it is one of the town's administration buildings.

41 Barfüßerkirche

The church of a former Franciscan monastery, first mentioned in 1243. With the Reformation it was taken over by the Lutheran preachers and is today a Protestant parish church. Originally a Gothic building of 1398, it was revamped in baroque style in the 18th century and destroyed in 1944. Inside there are valuable works of art among which are the blessing Christ Child and a crucifix by Georg Petel. The cloister features Late Gothic star-patterned reticulate vaulting.

42 Lech-Canals

From Roman times, the branched-off Lech canals south of Augsburg have given the Lech quarter its name and character and the typical course of the lanes. The abundant flow of water served the craftsmen and mills not only with the necessary power, but was also used for cleaning and refuse disposal in the confined quarters of the old town.

43 Old Silver Smithy

One-time silver smithy of the late 15th century, with a typical outside wooden staircase to the upper storey. Restored and used as a silver smithy again.

44 Crafts and guilde walk

The Augsburg Crafts and Guilds Walk, which is to date unique, leads the visitor through the old town areas in Germany, through the Lech quarter between the City Hall and Rotes Tor.

Idyllic canals meander through the Lech quarter like a network, partly subterranean, partly open. Craftsmen had settled along this arm of the Lech from the Middle Ages using water power as a source of energy. Some of these objects remain today together with the craftsmen's workshops.

45 Dominikanerkirche

Roman museum. Dominikaner-gasse 15. A church of the former monastery of St. Magdalena with a double nave and stucco work of the Feichtmayr brothers (1720). Pre-historic, Roman times and the Early Middle Ages are on display. Open Wednesday through Sunday from 10 a.m. to 4 p.m.

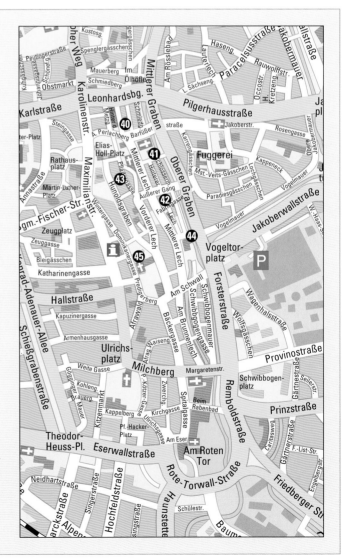

MAXIMILIANMUSEUM

New Approaches to Augsburg's History

Despite severe war damage, Augsburg, as the capital city of Bavarian-Swabia, still possesses historical districts, squares and buildings that bear authentic testament to the imperial glory of this ancient municipality.

These monuments left a permanent impression on Stefan Zweig. In 1930, the author wrote enthusiastically about an early morning walk through Augsburg: "… as though through a different century, I walked past the palatial buildings, as, undisguised, they illuminated their massive beauty in growing light. All other sensations of the hour and the present lay still in slumber, only the past was awake with an urgency and elegant force that I have felt in hardly any other German city. Only the fountains spoke, adorned with elegant forms, only the painted houses gave word and voice."

Of the Augsburg civic palaces that impressed Zweig so deeply, the Maximilian Museum, located in the city's historic centre, is one of the few not to be destroyed in the war. Philippine-Welser-Straße, which is dominated by the magnificent Renaissance façade of the Maxi-

milian Museum, was originally a square called Alter Heumarkt. Now it is part of the extensive pedestrian precinct, with its numerous book dealers, shops and department stores.

The majestic civic palace is proclaimed by banners and a six-metre-long concrete bench bearing the characteristic legend MAXIMILIANMUSEUM. The "municipal furniture" invites you to linger in the busy shopping street, and arouses your curiosity about the associated old-Augsburg patrician's house, a building complex consisting of two late-Gothic and Renaissance town houses. Its residents have written Augsburg and European history. By looking at the past, we can see that the building's current use, as a museum of art and cultural history, is ideally in keeping with its historic significance.

From 1515 to 1519, the rear house on Annastraße was occupied by the Augsburg patrician Bartholomäus Welser (1484–1561), and is known as the Welser House in his honour. Bartholomäus was head of the Welser trading company from 1519. Together with Jakob Fugger the Wealthy, he bankrolled the election

of Charles V as Holy Roman Emperor – a decision of global historic importance for Europe, Germany and the Imperial City. The striking effigies of these two representatives of the "Golden Augsburg" of the Renaissance are displayed in the Maximilian Museum in the form of two contemporary portrait medals. Among the Welser trading company's most audacious enterprises was to acquire monopoly trading rights in Venezuela and brutally plunder the country, protected by privileges of Charles V. The trading company lost its rights in 1556 with the abdication of Charles.

The, "massive", to use Stefan Zweig's word, main building on Philippine-Welser-Straße was built at the beginning of the 1540s by the Augsburg trader, banker and counsellor to the emperor, Leonhard Beck of Beckenstein. The Imperial City, which had given its name to the "Confessio Augustana", the confession of faith of the Protestant Estates of the Empire proclaimed at the Diet of 1530, was a purely Protestant city at that time. It was in confrontation with the Emperor, its foremost patron, who still followed the old faith. With this building, which was extraordinarily magnifi-

cent even by Augsburg standards, Beck of Beckenstein, a Catholic, now introduced himself as one of the Emperor's true party liners. The façade ornamentation, which was restored at the end of the 1970s, shows a base painted with sgraffito diamond rustications on the ground floor, with the first and second floors subdivided by pilasters. The ornamentation of the two oriels, besides Renaissance motifs such as putti and tendrils, shows portrait medals of Roman and Habsburg emperors, testifying to its builder's humanist scholarship. The zenith of the imperial iconography on the right-hand oriel is represented by the imperial double eagle and the device of Charles V, and pillars of Hercules with the motto "plus ultra" – "ever onward".

The stately building, costing a good 20,000 gulden, became a fiasco for Beck. He got into such debt that only his business partner Jakob Her-

brot (ca. 1493–1564), Augsburg's last guild mayor, could release him from the financial trap. Herbrot had gained enormous wealth through trading in luxury goods and credit business. Beck had to sign over the building to Herbrot, and when he refused to leave the house that he had only just occupied, Herbrot took him before the city court in 1547 for non-fulfillment of the loan agreement, and he was ordered to move out. That was bad enough for Beck. But on top of it, Herbrot was a Protestant. As Augsburg's mayor, he took the Imperial City into the Schmalkaldic War against the Emperor.

After Charles V had won a victory over the Protestants in 1547 at the battle of Mühlberg, he held a tribunal against them in Augsburg at the famous 1548 Diet, the "Geharnischter Reichstag". Herbrot had only just moved into his new domicile on the Alter Heumarkt, whose

magnificence also impressed the members of the Diet. To the annoyance of Beck, Charles V did not make any moves to drive the "enemy of the state" Herbrot out of his house, let alone – to Beck's even greater regret – condemn him to death. Instead, an exorbitant ransom was imposed on the rich Augsburg trader – at the Diet, they spoke of 60,000 gulden! In 1551, Herbrot's good contacts to the House of Habsburg were rewarded when he was appointed royal counsellor by Charles' brother King Ferdinand I. Herbrot's politics against Charles V had also made a significant contribution to the Emperor's decree of a new constitution for Augsburg in 1548, The "Carolingian Municipal Code", which lasted until 1806 and is preserved in the Maximilian Museum in the form of a heraldic chart painted on parchment, like an organigram. The new constitution took power away from the guilds and gave the leading political role to the patricians. The two mayors, now patricians, were known as Stadtpfleger from now on. The Catholics were restored to their old rights, following years in exile. From then on, Augsburg was a biconfessional city. This status was confirmed by the Augsburg Religious Peace, which was proclaimed at the Diet of 1555 in the old Gothic town hall, a model of which, created in 1615 shortly before it was demolished, is preserved in the Maximilianmuseum. With the Augsburg Religious Peace, the Augsburg confession was acknowledged once and for all in imperial law, and the ecclesiastical split in the Empire was thereby codified.

The highs and lows of the coexistence of Catholics and Protestants in the Imperial City of Augsburg are typified by the biography of the important Augsburg art agent and Protestant Philipp Hainhofer (1578 – 1647), who spent his childhood in the house on Alter Heumarkt. The main building of the Maximilian Museum is named Hainhofer House after him. Hainhofer, who also operated internationally as a diplomat, was in contact with many German and European princes, and brokered many objets d'art, manufacture of which was a speciality in the Imperial City. An outstanding example from this time is Georg Petel's outstanding ivory tankard of 1630, decorated with a bacchanal, which has been joined by Death in the form of the Grim Reaper. This work, which was created in the middle of the Thirty Years War, is one of the Museum's greatest treasures. For the Protestant Duke Philipp von Pommern-Stettin, Hainhofer designed the famous Pommerscher

Kunstschrank (Pommeranian collectors' cabinet), which was destroyed in the Second World War. At the same time, however, the Augsburgers also enjoyed the confidence of the Catholic Duke Maximilian I of Bavaria, who gained the electoral dignity of Palatine in 1619 following his victory over the Calvinist "Winter King" Friedrich V of the Palatinate. As part of the restitution edict issued by Emperor Ferdinand II in 1629, Hainhofer was dismissed as a Protestant councillor along with

many other Protestants in municipal offices who refused to adopt the Catholic religion. The consequence of the restitution edict, which also led to the dismissal of all Protestant preachers in Augsburg are still remembered by the "Augsburger Hohe Friedensfest" (Peace Festival), a public holiday only for the city of Augsburg, has been celebrated annually since 1650 to this day. In 1632, King Gustav Adolf II of Sweden took possession of the Imperial City and restored the Protestants to

Left: View of the city history department with a portrait of King Gustav Adolf and city chronicle. Right: Georg Petel, ivory tankard showing a bacchanal, Augsburg, ca. 1630.

their offices and rights, while the Catholics were paid back in their own coin. In the same year, the imperial court painter Matthäus Gundelach produced a full-length life-size portrait of the Swedish King for the Protestant Augsburg patrician family Thenn – one of the jewels of the municipal history department of the Maximilian Museum. After the defeat of the Swedes at the battle of Nördlingen, the tide turned again in 1634. Siege and starvation, which are commemorated in the Maximilian Museum by a corn measurers' silver guild cup bearing cautionary words, were followed by further suppression of the Protestant population by the occupying imperial troops. Hainhofer did not live to see the end of the negotiations between Münster and Osnabrück; he died in 1647 – one year before the Augsburg Protestants received their rights and churches back again with the Westphalian Peace of 1648. To re-equip the churches, altar furniture was commissioned from the Augsburg goldsmiths. Impressive testaments to this are two items in the Maximilian Museum on loan from the Lutheran

Barfüßerkirche – a Last Supper sketch and a tabernacle from 1649. The Westphalian Peace brought parity to the Imperial City, the coequal staffing of all municipal offices, right up to the Stadtpfleger, with a Catholic and a Protestant.

At the end of the 17th century, the house on the Alter Heumarkt was occupied by the Augsburg copper-plate engraver and publisher Elias Christoph Heiß, son of the Protestant superintendent Johann Georg and great nephew of the painter Johann Heiß. As one of the first copper engravers in Southern Germany, he used the novel, painterly mezzo-tint technique, and besides portrait engravings also specialised in large-format "thesis engravings". The highly successful Augsburg art publisher acquired an important collection. He had the gallery for his collection of paintings decorated with a ceiling fresco by the Tyrolean artist Melchior Steidl, pupil of the

Munich court painter J. A. Gumpp. It shows scenes from the Roman poet Virgil's Aeneid. Now, it houses the heart of the Maximilian Museum's sculpture collection, which the city acquired in 1924 from the Munich privy councillor Sigmund Röhrer and contains small baroque sculptures and drafts, so-called "bozzetti", mainly from South Germany. The acquisition of this important collection marks the birth of the Augsburg art collections. The Catholic Steidl is among the early South German fresco painters, who transplanted the high-baroque, Roman quadratura panting to South Germany. Among his chief works are the imperial hall of the Bamberg Residence. On the 1st floor of the Maximilian Museum, Steidl created the ceiling fresco with the allegory of night for Heiß's former bedroom. This room now belongs to the department of scientific instruments, and contains valuable astronomical implements from the work-

Top: Melchior Steidl, ceiling fresco with allegory of night, ca. 1700.
Centre: in the sculpture collection of the Maximilian Museum.
Right: Corn measurers' guild cup, silver, engraved, gold plated, Augsburg, 1643.

shop of the famous Augsburg precision mechanic Georg Friedrich Brander (1713–1783), who was a highly respected member of numerous royal academies of science. Steidl's masterpiece is the great ceiling fresco in the festival hall on the 2nd floor, which shows the ancient heaven of the Gods and the four continents. Here can be found the glory of the Museum's collection – the department of Augsburg goldsmithery, whose decoration is thanks to the freeman of Augsburg, Kurt F. Viermetz and his wife Felicitas. The Felicitas Room, named after the great patroness of the Maximilian Museum provides an authentic historical setting for a magnificent presentation of baroque silver furniture, and dinner and dressing-table services – masterpieces of the Augsburg goldsmiths who were famous for their skill.

From 1706, the building complex of the current Maximilian Museum

was home to the venerable Protestant Armenkinderhaus (home for poor children) for almost 150 years. When, in 1731/1732, Salzburg emigrants came top Augsburg in their thousands, some of them also settled in the house on the Alter Heumarkt. Towards the end of the 18th century, a neighbour, the Protestant silver dealer Johann Gottlieb Klaucke (1719–1805), originally from Kustrin, played an enthusiastic part in the fate of the Armenkinderhaus by bequeathing it a huge sum of over 400,000 gulden. As silver dealer who was active throughout Europe, Klaucke, in 1780, had brokered one of the most sensational commissions of the 18th century for the Augsburg gold and silversmiths, namely to supply a total of six dinner services for the Russian Tsarina Katherine the Great. They were intended for various newly established administrations of her huge empire. Each service was intended for 40 persons and contained over 1,000 parts, and was crafted à la mode – in the latest classical taste preferred by the Tsarina. A few years before the fall of the ancien régime, and therefore also of the Imperial City, which had been the leading goldsmith metropolis of Central Europe in the 17th and 18th centuries, the large order from the Tsarina proved once again its unique capabilities and qualities as a supplier to the courts of Europe. The art collections have been able to acquire important pieces on the international art market since 1990. After the Armenkinderhaus, renamed "Klauckehaus", had moved into up-do-date, modern quarters in the north of the city, the Augsburg City Council decided to purchase the building on the Alter Heumarkt in 1853 to establish a municipal museum. It was opened in 1855. The following year, fifty years after the end of imperial immediacy, King Maximilian II of Bavaria permitted the city to name the house "Maximilian Museum" in his honour.

Since its foundation, the headquarters of Augsburg's art collections and museums has frequently made fundamental changes to its profile, its collections and its presentation. The most recently completed redesign of the display rooms, with about 1,700 m² exhibition area, was prompted by the comprehensive structural renovation of the house between 1998 and 2002. The museum received a completely new infra-

Top: Augsburg dinner set for the courts of Europe in the Felicitas hall. Right: The model chamber with unique architectural and technical models from the Renaissance and baroque.

structure with thermostat systems, new security technology, toilets and barrier-free routing of visitors. A functional and convenient opening up of access to the different floors, with spacious staircases and a lift, was also overdue. In 2003, the noble entrance hall of the main building received a modern service area with cash desk, museum shop and an enticing reading café. The building now has a room for revolving exhibitions, the Welser Hall, with lecture room and an information hall for the history of the house. A highlight of the modernisation of the Maximilian Museum is the self-supporting glass roof of the interior courtyard. Elaborately restored original sculptures from the Augsburg

show fountains were installed here in the 1990s.

Commissioned by the city in 1600, these statues by the famous court sculptors Hubert Gerhard and Adriaen de Vries – the "elegant forms" admired by Zweig – are among the Maximilian Museum's greatest treasures, and represent an internationally unique collection. The programme of statues of the Augustus, Mercury and Hercules Fountains, with its wealth of allusions, glorifies Augsburg as a city founded by the Romans that can look back at over 1,600 years of history; which as a free imperial city was only subject to the emperor, and as a metropolis of commerce and art was among the leading cities in the Holy Roman Empire, indeed in Europe. Augsburg's fountain statues, which can claim to be world cultural heritages, are a unique example of how the art of a religiously split citizenry can communicate

shared "ideology-free" values: pride in Augsburg's Roman history, in its importance as an international trading metropolis and in its sovereignty as a free imperial city guaranteed by the emperor.

The restoration and installation of these fountain statues was an unparalleled combined tour de force by various state and municipal offices, private foundations and individual citizens. Typical of those staunchly committed to the project are the Augsburg free citizens Kurt F. Viermetz and his wife Felicitas, both of whom, with a private donation of DM 1.5 million made possible the construction of the prize-winning high-tech glass roof. This literally central area, which is freely accessible to all visitors, has been named the Viermetzhof in their honour. Both a visiting card and nameplate for the new Maximilian Museum, it also points the way for the reconception and reopening of the outstanding collections, since visitors to the Maximilian Museum entering the 30 newly designed rooms with their total of 1,300 exhibits, are embarking on a time-trip through the artistic, cultural and municipal history of the Imperial City of Augsburg. Some 200 years after the end of its status as Imperial City, and its assignment to Bavaria, Augsburg now stands at the centre of the reconceived Maximilian Museum.

Like the magnificent bronze sculptures in the Viermetzhof, there are also other important departments of the Maximilian Museum with roots in the Imperial City, and which can now be visited and experienced again. They include, for example the unique model chamber from the Rathaus, assembled over four centuries, which is now listed as a national heritage. Nowhere else in the world is there a comparable collection of architectural and technical models in this quality and quantity, including the famous model by the City Architect Elias Holl for rebuilding the Augsburg Rathaus between 1615 and 1620. Other items of cultural importance are the architectural and mechanical models and model mills, mainly from the 18th century. They illustrate the high technical standard of water supply, for which the Imperial City was once so famous. Also exhibited are artefacts of the Reichsstädtische Kunstakademie (imperial city art academy), which, with its important directors, greatly influenced the direction of art in Augsburg and South Germany in the 18th century. The department of scientific instruments, together with the important collection of the St. Anna high school, founded in 1531, and the city library, which has existed since 1537, contains outstanding works by famous Augsburg watch and compass makers, the "Mechanici". By the end of imperial immediacy, Augsburg had been able to maintain its excellent reputation as the "Schule aller Mechanicorum" (school of mechanics) (Leibniz). In addition, there are some minor collections, such as those from the former arsenal.

A characteristic feature of Augsburg and the Maximilian Museum links together the bronzes in the Viermetzhof and the Museum's other superlative collections. They are the works of art that bring Augsburg's history to life in a quite unique way. Art distinguished this city and made it unique. In the 17th and 18th centuries, Augsburg was the production centre for art in the Empire and the centre of art export spreading to Europe. Its special feature was the unique variety of the artistic professions practised here. The most important craft for many of the over 60 professional artists who settled here was gold and silver smithing. The Imperial City saw itself essentially as a city of the arts. This is clearly shown by the department of Augsburg craftsmanship, which presents a fascinating wealth of precious products, such as the Augsburg house painters, pewter founders, faïence potters, joiners and watchmakers. The terms "Imperial City" and "art" were inseparable for Augsburg. The Imperial City of Augsburg, as sensed by Stefan Zweig in his morning walk among the fountains and buildings, is no longer a presence. But the new Maximilian Museum is a place where memory remains ever present and vital, and a visit can become an unforgettable experience. The house, completely reopened at the end of 2006, has developed into one of Augsburg's great attractions and a meeting place beloved by both locals and outsiders. Augsburg meets itself here and it is here we find Augsburg.

The Maximilian Museum received the Bavarian Museum Award in 2007.

DRIVING FORCES
FOR AUGSBURG

Augsburg is a city of water. The Romans chose this site 2000 years ago, on a spur of land between the rivers Lech and Wertach, which spring from the mountains. They conjoin within view of the former Roman city of Augusta Vindelicum. The occupying forces were already using the rivers as transport routes. Even centuries later, when Augsburg became an episcopal Imperial City in the middle ages, their waters still bore many thousands of rafts, carrying, besides timber, a range of freights – stones, lime, gypsum, charcoal, wool bales, livestock wind and victuals of all kinds.

The Lech formed an important transport artery, and the powerful engine for a blooming economy. The canals that were diverted from the Lech drove the water wheels for corn and hammer mills. Since mediaeval times, water had been an indispensable energy supplier for a large number of crafts and played a significant role in Augsburg's prosperity. The water courses created centuries ago still pass through the former crafts and factory quarter. You can follow them for long stretches and cross them over hundreds of bridges. Sometimes they disappear under houses and roads, branch and unite again. Water crossings are an unusual feature. Canals cross one another here without their waters mixing.

The Augsburgers were always aware of the importance of water for their city. That is why they embodied their rivers Lech, Wertach, Singold and Brunnenbach as statues on the Augustus Fountain, built in 1594. The river allegories recline as female and male nudes on the edge of the basin. While the Lech and Wertach served as water routes for the rafts, and also filled the city canals, the Singold, in 1588 for example, drove no fewer than 38 mill wheels outside the city. However, the Brunnenbach, honoured with a bronze statue, had another function that was no less important – it supplied Augsburg with drinking water for over 400 years, and from 1599 fed the Augustus, Mercury and Hercules fountains.

Water has Spouted from Fountains since 1412

Until 1412, drinking water in Augsburg was obtained from crank, draw or bucket wells. But these wells, which were available at numerous places around the city were not fountains. At the beginning of the 15th century, the city council wanted "spouting water" from fountains in the city centre. But this required flowing water, which was only available in the workers' districts below the high terrace. The houses of the well-to-do, the Rathaus, episcopal palace and monasteries were several metres above the levels of the canals and streams, and water had to be carried up to them. That was a huge technical problem 600 years ago.

In 1412, the Augsburger Leopold Karg took the plunge and installed fountains to splash away up on the high class squares and streets. At the city moat, in front of Schwibbogentor, one of the city gates, he built a pump, which was driven by a water wheel, and conveyed water into a tank on a tower. From this elevated container, it descended again in a pipe and flowed by its own pressure uphill to public fountain tanks. The first was set up at the Rathaus, and the second in front of Weberhaus. However, Leopold Karg had no experience in conveying water. The forged iron pipes proved too narrow. Augsburg's first water pipe did not operate satisfactorily. Moreover, the Imperial City deemed the costs too high. It fell into dispute with Leopold Karg. However, they still liked the idea of city fountains and looked for an experienced master of fountains.

He was found in 1416 in the person of Nördlingen-born Hans Felber. He built a new

The Lech has served its purpose as a transport route, but its water is more in demand than ever for power generation: a large number of generators are producing "Lech electricity".

water pumping station with a wooden tower near the Rotes Tor. He replaced the iron pipes with hollowed-out pine trunks. His system of supplying the fountains worked. A contemporary described it as "exquisite, useful and good". The citizens of the Imperial City to have flowing water before many other important cities.

The drinking water flowing into the fountains came from the woods near the Lech and meadows in the south, well away from the city. Here, there were many natural springs. The Brunnenbach was developed into a "water reservoir" and supplied the relatively pure water at the Rotes Tor to the sumps. At the same point, the less clean Lochbach was led into the city separately from this. Its purpose was to drive the pumps that conveyed the valuable drinking water into reservoirs at the top of the fountain towers.

The wooden fountain tower erected in 1416 at the Rotes Tor burned down in 1464, making clear how dependent the city was on a single pumping system. A second tower was therefore built in 1470 next to the Neubau, which was now made of stone. The waterworks became a trinity when a city wall tower was rebuilt as the well tower in 1599. Two floors were added to it to increase the pressure, and supplied the Augustus Fountain, which was built in 1594, the Mercury Fountain installed from 1599, and fed the 21 fountains of the Hercules complex from 1602. To supply further city districts with flowing water, a disused defence tower on Mauerberg was rebuilt as a fountain tower in 1450. In 1609, the City Master of Works Elias Holl built two water towers at the edge of Jakobervorstadt between the Jakobertor and Oblatterwall.

For 80 years, the water towers only supplied public fountains. In 1502, the prince bishop received the first private connection; the second was acquired by the Benedictine Abbey of St. Ulrich and Afra a year later. From 1545, Anton, Hans Jakob and Georg Fugger were supplied with free "piped water" because of their manifold services to the city. It was only in 1558, when the water supply was significantly expanded, that everyone was able to have flowing water in their house – provided they were rich enough to afford this special luxury. A "pipe" of water (around 150 litres per hour) from the city supply cost 200 golden gulders as a one-off payment, or 10 gulden per year.

Expensive Spring Water from Bavaria

To the misfortune of the Augsburgers, their water catchment area lay outside the territory of the Imperial City. The headwaters, from which most of the drinking water still comes, belong to Bavaria. Until 1806, the Free Imperial City saw Bavaria as a foreign country that was only rarely friendly. Most of the impecunious Bavarian dukes and prince electors knew how to exploit the Swabian Imperial City's dependence and charged heavily for the water taken from their domains. Put simply, they blackmailed the Augsburgers. What choice did they have but to pay to have the vital clean drinking water piped into the city?

In 1602, the Imperial City had exchanged the present Siebentischwald of the bishop for the property more distant from the city. This 260-hectare wood close to the city was only a corridor area for the wellsprings located even further south, and the Lochbach, derived from

The Hercules fountain has been spouting water since 1602 from artistic bronze gargoyles, created by Adriaen de Vries.

the Lech. The damming of the Lech, which formed the border with Bavaria, the rafting, the diversion of Lech water into the city canals and the tapping of drinking water led to frequent disputes with the Bavarian sovereigns. Augsburg did have several imperial charters from 1418 for leading the Lech into the city through as many streams as necessary. But that didn't worry the ruling Wittelsbachers in Munich. Their coffers were chronically empty. They therefore sought for additional sources of revenue and were only too ready to exploit the wealthy Imperial City on the other side of the Lech as a cash cow. In 1470, two bishops adjudicated in the water disputes between Duke Albrecht IV and Augsburg. Some 4,000 gulden in gold went to the residence city of Munich in this settlement. In 1516, there were agreements about new obstructions on the Lech; in 1558 there was a serious quarrel with Duke Albrecht V of Bavaria. Among other things, the Imperial City had dared to acquire further sources in Meringer-

au without prior discussion. For the "gracious settlement" in the contentious questions of water, Augsburg had to pay 50,000 gulden. The Lech actually formed the frontier between Bavaria and the Imperial City. But the wooded area of Meringerau, with its many springs, was Bavarian territory on the Swabian side of the river boundary. This was because the Lech had changed its course eastwards. Around 300 AD, it still flowed very close to Haunstetten and Augsburg. After extreme dry periods or floods, it suddenly shifted its main course to the east. The Bavarians still referred to the old course as the legally valid boundary in their territorial claims. That is why Meringerau, which comprised the territory of Siebenbrunn and the Haunstetter Wald, was under Bavarian sovereignty.

The Imperial City would have been only too pleased to purchase the wooded and meadow area, but Bavaria was never willing – after all, Augsburg would then no longer have been open to blackmail. The contrasts therefore had to be renewed in 1623 with Duke William and in 1642 with Elector Maximilian. When Elector Max Emanuel was in serious need of

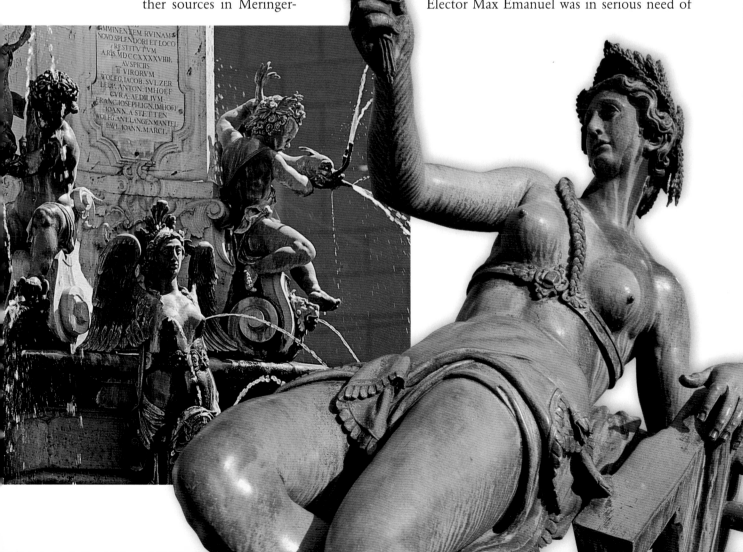

money again in 1721, he mortgaged the entire Meringerau, "with all waters therein" to the Imperial City for 40 years against a loan of 100,000 gulden. In 1763, Augsburg had to renounce the repayment of the loan and pay another 60,000 gulden for the continued use of the springs in Meringerau. In 1806, Augsburg lost its imperial immediacy and was incorporated into the Kingdom of Bavaria, newly created by Napoleon. Since then, the city has been able to purchase as much area as it wants in its drinking water catchment area.

Waterworks as a Jewel of Industrial Architecture

However, the problems of providing pure drinking water didn't get easier after 1806. For reasons of hygiene, the city saw itself forced to use surface water in the first half of the 19th century. Collector wells were built at the water towers, and drinking water was taken from them. Stream water now only served to drive the pumps. Despite technical improvements and turbine drives, it was not possible to supply the fast-growing city adequately. In 1878, the five pumps only supplied 6,000 cubic metres per day. Only 877 of 3,368 Augsburg properties and 68 public fountains were connected to the pipe network, which supplied water rated partly as "good" and partly as "dangerously infiltrated". Almost 75 percent of the 57,200 residents at that time received their supplies from 1,265 pump wells, which were predominantly "horribly contaminated", it was reported at the time. The consequences, with several cholera and typhus epidemics, were catastrophic. Many people died. It dawned on many of those responsible that uncontaminated drinking water was the most important factor in public health. In 1876, after long preparations, the decision was made for the most expensive, most radical, but also most farsighted solution to the drinking water problem – the creation of a waterworks at Siebentischwald and supply only from wells in this wooded area owned by the city.

Augsburg master builders, engineers and companies designed and built a waterworks at the Hochablasswehr ("high outlet" weir) with many technical innovations. The revolution was "towerless pumping", without the use of a water tower. Now, this has been replaced by four ten-metre-high pressurised tanks, into which the water was forced from three massive double pumps. Three turbines driven by Lech water, with a total of 296 horsepower, drove the powerful twin piston pumps. From the beginning of October 1879, ten million litres of crystal-clear water per day spurted at 5.5 bar pressure into the 55-centimetre diameter mains pipe. It was distributed via a 54-kilometre pipe network through the entire municipal area. Every property owner was now obliged to connect to the system. The old water supply from the towers in the city area that had been in operation since 1416 was shut down. After a few years, the old technical facilities were removed.

The Augsburg-manufactured piston pumps that were brought into operation in 1879 ran for 94 years with water drive. The Lech supplied the energy for the turbines. In December 1973, the powerful pumps were shut down. Electric motors and modern centrifugal pumps finally took on the jobs of the extremely dependable, robust machinery, which had drawn experts from all over the world to Augsburg for decades after it started opera-

Three well towers at the Rotes Tor supplied drinking water until 1879. Together with the Stadttor and Bastion, they form a unique historic ensemble.

tion. Over 100 years after its creation, the model waterworks was in need of renovation. The exterior of the twin-towered water works was renovated in 1986; however, the interior of the 37-metre-long, 17.5-metre-wide hall is a sober, uniform green-grey. This colour only changed in 1990, when the removal of the old roller blinds revealed intensely colourful old paintwork. An extensive study clarified the situation – two paint coats concealed fantastic decorative paintings, such as friezes and marine animals, as well as palmette motifs, covering parts of the walls and ceiling. Restoration began in 1993. Square meter by square meter, the former brightly designed hall of the utility building was transformed back into a treasure. Since the closure of the old, completely preserved pumping equipment, the waterworks had been an eminent technical museum. Now it was to be a late-classicist jewel of industrial architecture.

A Thousand Rafts for Augsburg

The use of Lech water for pumping drinking water was the most recent and shortest chapter in the utilisation of the Lech. The tradi-

tional functions of the river originating in the Alps have been evoked at the Hochablass-wehr since 1912 by two stone sculptures – a "spinstress" with spindle, cornucopia and turbines is intended to symbolise industry; a powerful man can be recognised as a rafter by his attributes of axe and rope. Water power and rafting have brought prosperity to the city for decades and the "high outlet" had two purposes from time immemorial – The most important was the diversion of sufficient water into the canals to drive waterwheels. The watercourses are still called "Lech" [Vorderer (front), Mittlerer (middle) and Hinterer (rear) Lech, Schwalllech and Sparrenlech], and the district through which they flow is the "Lechviertel". This is where most of the mills and artisans' shops were located, which were powered by undershot wooden paddle wheels.

The hygienic importance of the water, rushing in some places but in others only splashing or murmuring, must not be underestimated. For centuries, all the city rubbish landed in it, from the contents of the chamber pots to the butchers' waste. Sewer pipes still discharged into the city canals around 1900, which in turn flowed into the Lech. The excess water from the constantly flowing drinking water line flushed the drains. This type of waste disposal was considered exemplary for a long time. Augsburg became famous as a clean city.

The Lech was already a transport route for Augsburg in the middle ages, and indispensable as an energy source and sewer. The Hochablass at the Lech was therefore designed so that rafts can sail into Stadtbach and, from there, can turn off into Kaufbach, Herrenbach and Proviantbach. That is where the large wood storage areas, and company landing places and berths are located. Rafts not destined for Augsburg passed through the raft channel.

In 1580, 2,870 rafts were destined for Augsburg, in 1610 it was about 3,000. The year 1865 as gone down in history as the zenith, with 4,332 watercraft. Many rafts carried freight – up to 12 cattle or 60 barrels of gypsum or 100 hundredweight of zinc could be loaded. About a half of the rafts reaching the Hochablass sailed past Augsburg to further down the Lech and Danube. By the way, until 1850 you could reach Augsburg by "ordinary raft" almost to a timetable.

Between 1880 and 1890, there was still an average of over 1,800 rafts and "Flitschen", i.e. plank rafts. In 1900, there were 1,107; four years later 630 and in 1908, only 134; in 1910 there were only 11 rafts and 10 plank rafts. The wooden Hochablasswehr had proved its mettle against many floods, but in 1910 there was a catastrophe. Snow melting in the mountains and cloudbursts caused a massive flood wave from 14th June, which washed away the weir, canal lock and restoration building. The canals were dry. The Hochablass had to be rebuilt as fast as possible; the city needed Lech water. The work began in February 1911. On July 28, 1912, a state-of-the-art weir together with a ten-metre-wide raft channel and an extended raft harbour could start service. On November 8, 1912, the first two long-distance rafts passed through the new raft channel on the trip from Lechbruck to Regensburg. At this time, rafting was no longer important. When, on June 9, 1914, the Bavarian royal couple visited the new Hochablass, the city organised a "show trip" of two rafts ordered in Prem at the Lech overflow. This day counts as the end of Lech rafting in Augsburg.

Water Power as an Engine of Industry

"The great hydraulic power was of fundamental importance for the emergence and growth of Augsburg industry", was the conclusion of a study about the reasons for the city's economic boom from 1835. As early as 1276, water drove the ten grain mills in the city mentioned by name; water remained Augsburg's primary energy supplier until about 1900. That is shown by statistics – in 1761, on the canals and streams, there were 78 waterworks with a total of 163 wheels. The undershot paddle wheels only used about 20 percent of the driving force. Grain mills therefore required between four and eight wheels for milling. Waterwheels drove the stamping hammers in paper mills and tobacco manufacturing, wood turning machines, smithing hammers and the fulling for dyers and bleachers.

While the relatively low power of waterwheels was adequate for artisans' workshops,

Since 1902, the electricity works at Wolfzahnau has delivered environmentally friendly electricity generated with Lech water. It has long enjoyed a high reputation as a "living industrial monument".

water power played a subordinate role in Augsburg's early industrial development in the late 18th and early 19th century. That was because the old low-efficiency wheels did not supply enough energy. That changed suddenly with the invention of the turbine (the first came from France in the 1830s). Now Augsburg's wealth of flowing water attracted the attention of many major textile companies.

In 1840, 126 factories with 230 wheels or turbines were exploiting water power in the city. That represented the absolute peak. Proviantbach, Hanreibach, Fichtelbach, Sparrenlech, Stadtbach and Schäfflerbach were enlarged into "industrial canals". From 1830, the abundance of water in Augsburg led to the building of many new factories here. The worsted yarn spinning mill from Nuremberg transferred to Augsburg in 1836 purely because of the availability of water power. Other factories were founded on the great canals.

Improved technology permitted improvements in efficiency from year to year. In 1850, 203 water wheels or turbines generated 2,557 "dynamic horsepower"; within 15 years, the yield had doubled to almost 5,200 hp. In 1902, there were only 69 water machines operating on the Lech canals, though by now they were delivering 10,680 hp.

Around 1890, Lech and canal water began to be used to generate electrical power in Augsburg. The city's abundance of natural resources in the form of water, its elixir of life and guarantee of its prosperity for many centuries, received a new, more sustainable task. Now, water is generating more electricity than ever in the city area, and the number of power generators is increasing.

Reproduction water wheels at Vogeltor and Schwibbogengasse continue to remind us of the ancient technology. The "Lechs" still rush past the houses in the old city alleyways. Testaments to the early history of drinking water are everywhere to see. They are five former reservoir towers: three at the Rotes Tor, one rectangular tower above the Unterer Graben (whose former pump house at Bei den Sieben Kindeln now houses a cinema) and the "Unterer Jakober Brunnenturm" on the city moat at Oblatterwall.

**The Schaezler Palace and the State Gallery
of Old Masters in St. Katharine's Church –
Highlights of the Kunstsammlungen und
Museen Augsburg**

Kunstsammlungen und Museen Augsburg gathers together seven museums of different orientations under one roof – the Roman Museum in the Dominican Church, the Natural History Museum in the Augusta Arcades, The Deutsche Baroque Gallery, and the Karl-und-Magdalene-Haberstock foundation in the Schaezler Palace – with the attached State Gallery of Old Masters in St. Katharine's Church, the Maximilian Museum in the Hainhofer and Welser Houses, Mozart House, the Neue Galerie in Höhmann House and the H2 Centre for Contemporary Art in the Glass Palace, with the State Gallery of Modern Art, which was opened in 2006. This complex offers a comprehensive view of the history of culture and natural history in the old Imperial City of Augsburg and its cultural history until the present.

SCHAEZLERPALAIS

DER KUNSTLER IM BILD

Schaezler Palace: a Banker's Residence

The Schaezler Palace was built from 1765 to 1770 as the residence of the banker and trader Benedikt Adam Liebert von Liebenhofen (1731–1810). The "city house" was formally opened by the family on April 28, 1770, by Marie Antoinette, who was staying in Augsburg on her pre-nuptial tour – she was to marry the French Dauphin in Paris, on May 16, 1770.

The descendants, Dr. Wolfgang Lorenz von Schaezler and his wife Hilda Sophia, donated the building to the city of Augsburg in 1958, on condition that it should only be used for cultural purposes. The Schaezler Palace now contains the Deutsche Baroque Gallery, the Graphic Collection, the Karl-und-Magdalene-Haberstock-Stiftung, as well as housing the direction and administration of the Augsburg museum complex. The magnificent building was restored and renovated between 2004 and 2006 at a cost of around 5.7 million euro. This extensive project was only possible thanks to the broad support of the City, the Free State of Bavaria, the World Monument Fund and a Schaezler Palace funding committee coordinated by Kurt F. Viermetz, Hubert Stärker and Dr. Georg Haindl. The restoration also included a reorganisation of the collection, which relocated the German Baroque Gallery on the first floor, while the Karl-und-Magdalene-Haberstock foundation are now displayed in the three presentation rooms on the second floor. The rooms connecting with the long enfilade are now used for alternating exhibitions assembled from in-house and external holdings. Next to the cash desk on the ground floor, a cafeteria has recently been installed and, with the help of the descendants of the family of Dr. Siedler von Schaezler in Scherneck, furnished with original Biedermeier furniture from the Schaezler holdings.

The **German Baroque Gallery** presents an outstanding collection of 17th and 18th century paintings. This exhibition is structured into thematic units that allow visitors to appreciate different aspects of baroque art. Here you can find the topics *"The Residents of the House"*, *"Johann Heinrich Schönfeld"*, *"Myth and History"*, *"Augsburg Academy"*, *"The Artist in the*

Top:
The German
Baroque Gallery.
Photo: Christina
Bleier

Right:
David Roentgen
(1743–1807),
grandfather
clock, Neuwied
ca. 1785;
permanent loan
from the Ernst-
von-Siemens
Cultural-
Foundation.
Photo: Kunst-
sammlungen
und Museen
Augsburg

Right: Giovanni Antonio Canal, called Canaletto, view of the Piazza San Marco in Venice, ca. 1735, one of the principal works of the Haberstock-Foundation (Kunstsammlungen und Museen Augsburg). Photo: Helmut Schreiber

Picture", *"Still Life"*, etc. The paintings and oil sketches are each presented against different wall colours, which in turn are derived from the original monochrome supraportal paintings, that is to say the four colours yellow, red, green and blue run through the presentation as colouristic threads.

An outstanding item of furniture is the monumental grandfather clock from the Roentgen workshop in Neuwied, acquired in 2006 with the support of the Ernst-von-Siemens-Art-Foundation. Recent research indicates that it does not originate from the possessions of the von Schaezler family, but had been acquired earlier by the Augsburg Prince Bishop Clemens Wenzeslaus for his castle in Koblenz. The modern article of musical furniture, demonstrating the skill of the 18th century ébénistes, can play four different pieces of music thanks to a built-in flute and cymbal mechanism. The grandfather clock, manufactured in 1785 and installed in the dining room thus, so to speak, leads us into the architectural pinnacle of the Schaezler Palace, the great festival hall, which, with its preserved original decoration, is among

the architectural jewels of the city of Augsburg. Around 95 % of the surface has been preserved in its original condition. Eminent artists such as the electoral Bavarian court stucco-master Franz Xaver Feichtmayer the Younger (1735–1803) and his brother Simpert (1732–1806), and the sculptor Placidius Verhelst (1727–1778) contributed to the decoration of the festival hall, just as much as the wall painter Gregorio Guglielmi (1714–1773), who painted the ceiling fresco with the subject *"Der Handel verbindet die Erdteile"* *(Trade Unites the Continents)*. The festival hall embraces a universal programme that incorporates the continents in the ceiling fresco, the seasons, signs of the zodiac and of the elements as symbols on the mirror frame, as well as the flora and fauna of the continents in the supraportals. This world-spanning programme reflects the all-embracing ideas of the baroque age and the universal Eurocentric claim to power extending to the garden, which is visible from the festival hall. The symmetrical quadripartite design with a central fountain has been reconstructed, so that the rococo structure of the architecture is also reflected in the cultivated natural sphere.

STAATSGALERIE ALTE MEISTER

The triangular room connecting to the festival hall in the Schaezler Palace, with remains of the original Augsburg-manufactured wall-covering forms the transition to the State Gallery of the Old Masters in the former St. Katherine's Church.

The opening of the State Gallery in the former St. Katharine's church on October 12, 1835 – still a year before the opening of the Pinakothek in Munich – represented the birth of the older sister of the Munich Pinakotheks. The concentration of the holdings here as a result of the succession of the House of Wittelsbach and the secularisation

dates back to an idea by the gallery director Johann Christian von Mannlich (1741–1822), who, even in 1806, foresaw the presentation of the extensive painting holdings from the Residences of Mannheim, Zweibrücken and Düsseldorf. The secularised St. Katharine's Church, a Dominican convent founded in 1239 was adapted for presentation of the artistic treasures.

A closed holding of German Old Masters from Swabia and Augsburg has been on show here since 1964, including the so-called "Basilica Cycle", a cycle of paintings representing the seven principal churches of Rome

CHRISTOF TREPESCH | 117

created between 1499 and 1504 for the capital hall of St. Katharine's church by Hans Holbein the Elder (ca. 1465–1524), Hans Burgkmair (1473–1531) and a master "L.F.". This cycle is among the outstanding masterworks of Old German painting, since its complex programme of pictures gives us a deep insight into the piety of the late middle ages. The cycle is based on an indulgence granted to the Augsburg Dominican sisters of St. Katharina in 1487. The indulgences granted to the pilgrims for visiting the seven principal churches of Rome could thus also be gained in Augsburg without the need to make the pilgrimage. The panels were donated by the convent residents, the daughters of important patrician families in Augsburg.

An outstanding work of international importance is doubtless Albrech Dürer's (1471–1528) portrait of Jakob Fugger the Wealthy (1459–1525) of around 1520 (see page 37), which shows the prosperous businessman in a fur coat and Venetian cap against a chalky blue ground. From 1510, Jakob Fugger was the sole head of the Fugger trading company, which owned the biggest bank in Europe at the time. In 1514, he was the first German businessman to be given the title Reichsgraf.

Lucas Cranach's (1472–1553) wood panel of Samson and Delilah of 1529, which used to hang in the Augsburg Rathaus, is one of the high points of the Old Masters' collection in St. Katharine's church, and may count as a moral about "feminine power". The picture shows the moment when Delila cuts off Samson's hair, robbing him of his invincibility. Cranach depicts Samson's incipient vulnerability by his disconnected physicality, his legs and arms appearing as set pieces in the pyramidal figure composition, while, in the background, the Philistines are coming to blind him.

The State Gallery in St. Katharine's church, with its specialisation in Augsburg and Bavarian-Swabia, can be considered as one of Bavaria's outstanding collections of late-mediaeval painting.

The Mozart portrait was created by Leonhard Posch in 1788 after the "living model". Posch's relief, which Mozart's son considered "the most perfect likeness" is now among the greatest treasures of the Augsburg Mozart collections.

"We are Mozart!" – Augsburg in the Mozart jubilee year 2006.

AUGSBURG AS MOZART CITY

Allegro: Godfather and Papa

Augsburg is a Mozart city! It's not just that there is evidence of people called Mozart living around Augsburg since the mid-15th century. In Augsburg itself, the journeyman bricklayer David Mozart, in 1643, was the first to gain civil rights. His grandson, Johann Georg Leopold, later to be Vice-Kapellmeister and court composer to the prince-archbishop of Salzburg, was born on November 14, 1719, in the "Mozart House" at Frauentorstraße 30, as the son of a bookbinder, and more importantly, as an Augsburger. During his life, Leopold maintained links of friendship with the city of his birth, and even had his Augsburg civic rights confirmed on 1748 and 1751. While in Salzburg, he maintained active musical relationships with the Heilig Kreuz monastery, the Collegium musicum, a circle of more or less gifted amateur and professional musicians, who performed many of his works, and with the music publisher Johann Jakob Lotter, to whom Leopold entrusted the printing of his

musical legacy, the "Attempt at a Thorough Violin School" in 1756. No doubt about it. Leopold would have gone down in history, and not only Augsburg history, as one of the greatest music teachers and theoreticians of the 18th century! But on that memorable day of January 27, 1756, when he and his wife Anna Maria Pertl brought forth their darned seventh son, his rather thankless fate in the shadow of his son was sealed. "The boy is called Joannes Chrisostomus Wolfgang Gottlieb", so Leopold announced to Augsburg at the time. Nevertheless, shrewd Leopold soon recognised his child's special gifts, and organised a management that is still impressive to this day. Leopold was the only teacher – not only in musical matters – the boy ever had. He never attended a public school, by the way. Looking back affectionately at his Salzburg childhood, Wolfgang once noted "After God, Papa comes next; that was my motto as a child and I still stand by it." What followed was a short, shimmering life, full of highs and lows, which came to an end on December 5,

1791 at 55 past midnight by a "heated fever with rash".

But back to better times. The miracle "that God had caused to be born in Salzburg", visited "his Papa's home town" for the first time as a seven-year-old on June 22, 1763. "Herr Muzard mit Frau" lodged somewhat above their means at the Drei Mohren then, as now, the best hotel on Augsburg's Maximilianstraße. The lodgings, at 95 gulden, cost almost three times Leopold's monthly salary, by the way. The astute business-minded Swabian father presented the "six-year-old (!) clavicembalist from Salzburg" to an amazed public. What was described at the time as a special attraction – the child can "hear the sound of a bell ringing, or a clock, even a pocketwatch, strike" and name the precise note – was apparently not a concert, but one of those experimental shows so beloved at the time. It completely overstepped the borderline to a variety act when performances were given on a keyboard concealed by a "handkerchief". Who cares? Amidst cheers, the Mozart family circus continued its tour on July 7 to Mannheim

and all the important music metropolises of Western Europe. It was by no means a foregone conclusion that the celebrated wunderkind would later become the serious composer 'Wolfgang Amadé'. In 1777, Mozart requested his release from service at the Salzburg court orchestra to "try his luck elsewhere". On September 23, at around six o'clock, Mozart, with his mother (his father had not been granted a holiday), took his leave from Salzburg on a one-and-a-half year journey. What did they expect of it? Leopold, always the businessman, put it in a nutshell: "The purpose of the journey, the necessary purpose was, is, and must be, to receive a position or earn money." The electoral court in Munich, against the ambitious expectations, had proved ungracious; and so Augsburg was the next station on the trip.

Adagio I: Underpants and Handkerchiefs

After many disappointments and exasperations in Munich – the elector had given Mozart to understand that he should kindly first make his name in Italy – his hopes now turned to his father's birthplace and its (as

"A work that can be used" – Leopold Mozart's "Attempt at a Thorough Violin School" was first published in 1756 in the birth year of his son Wolfgang in Augsburg.

was mistakenly thought) art-infatuated patrician. Armed with all kinds of well-intentioned advice from his father … "If you do not have enough handkerchiefs, Augsburg is perhaps the best place to buy a half dozen or a dozen, but not blue ones, which lose their colour, or corrode the nose. The linen in Augsburg, too, will probably be the finest to have yourself two or at least one pair of underpants made" … Wolfgang Amadé stayed in Augsburg from October 11 to 26, 1777. To relieve the strain on his travel budget, seriously depleted after the Munich debacle, Leopold advised him by post to stay in the Weißes Lamm "in Heilige Kreuzergasse" this time, "where you pay 30 kreuzer per person and there are good rooms and even the respectable people, English, French, etc. stay". It was to be of greater significance that Leopold's brother Franz Aloisi – father of the famous "Bäsle" (female cousin) Maria Anna Thekla Mozart – lived "close by, namely in Jesuitengasse (house number 26)". But more about her later.

One of Wolfgang's first visits was to the famous organ and piano makers Johann Andreas Stein, a pupil of the even more famous Johann Andreas Silbermann in Strasbourg. Since the 1750s, Stein had increasingly dictated piano making; in 1773, he had succeeded in inventing a new escapement in Augsburg, which later created a furore as, regrettably, the "Viennese Action". The Mozarts maintained a long friendship with Johann Andreas Stein. Stein's "good Clavierl" had done the Mozarts "great service" as early as 1763 on their concert tours.

On October 12, 1777, Mozart, equipped with a friendly letter of recommendation from his father, set off for Steinhaus on Ulrichsplatz 10. Always ready for a joke, Wolfgang put on a pretence at first, and when Stein asked him if he was Mozart, he answered no: "O no, I said, I'm called Trazom, and have a letter (from father) for you. He took the letter and wanted to open it at once. But I didn't give him time and said, why do you want to read the letter now? Open up so that we can go into the chamber, for I am curious to see your piano forte… He opened up. I walked immediately to one of the three pianos that stood in

the room. I played, he could hardly open the letter, overtaken with eagerness, he only read the signature. Oh! he cried, and embraced me … and was just very satisfied." And Mozart was thrilled with Stein's forte pianos! Mozart had a less favourable opinion of Stein's daughter Nanette, who continually grimaced and gesticulated wildly while playing the piano.

What followed in the next two weeks was a tour of visits with, naturally, cultural accents: Just one of many highlights was the visit to the theatre built only the previous year in Lauterlech (which, like so many Augsburg Mozart sites, perished in the bombing in 1944), where, on the evening of October 14, the musical comedy "Der Teufel ist los" and the ballet "Der betrunkene Bauer" were shown, in which Emanuel Schickaneder was involved. The new establishment on the Lauterlech had already developed into a centre of German Mozart reverence – "Bastien and Bastienne" had already been performed here in 1777, and in 1780 the German ballad opera version of "La finta giardiniera" ("the pretended gar-

dener") was shown. "Don Giovanni" was performed in 1787, the same year as its première. In 1791, "Die Entführung aus dem Serail" (Abduction from the Seraglio) was performed and on January 21, 1793, with The Magic Flute, one of the first presentations of what is perhaps Mozart's most popular work, his joint venture with the "drunken peasant" Schickaneder. Organ trials followed in Barfüßerkirche (Stein's famous instrument was also destroyed in 1944), Soupé with improvised Fugue, also "arseling", for the connoisseur: "from behind, like a crab", in the Heilig Kreuz, a canon on "O you prick you, lick my arse" in St. Ulrich, compliments and honours from all side. Nowhere else had he been "heaped with so many tributes as here". And from the day of his arrival, his community of admirers made their pilgrimage to his lodgings in Heilig Kreuzer Gasse. Return in triumph to the city of his fathers! And it was just as well, since ultimately the travel costs had to be earned through concerts. His father's words of disapproval were already reaching from Salzburg to Augsburg: "You have spent too long in Munich and you must give one or two concerts in Augsburg if you are to earn anything, whether a little or a lot; the fine words, praise and bravissimos pay neither postmasters nor landlords."

No sooner said, than done … on October 12, the first day of his stay in Augsburg, Mozart went with his uncle in the morning to pay his respects to the powerful Catholic Stadtpfleger (as the mayor was called in Augsburg at the time), Jakob Wilhelm Langenmantel von Westheim und Ottmarshausen. Langenmantel had been a schoolfellow of Leopold Mozart at the Jesuit school and a fellow student at the University of Salzburg, and his memories of "his grace" were as bad as could be. Fate took its course: While the uncle had to wait "like a lackey" in the antechamber of Mr. "Longotabaro" (Langenmantel, "long coat"), Mozart was allowed to play "a good clavichord by Stein for almost three quarters of an hour in the presence of the stiff son and the spindly gracious young lady, and the simple old lady. Since Mozart hoped for a concert from the patricians, he also played for about an hour on the following day and was called on to appear again on the 14th at 11 o'clock for "musical entertainment". The young Langenmantel almost gave him to understand that nothing would become of the promised "Casino" (a concert before the patricians): "Came at around 11 o'clock. He gave me a lot of excuses. He said quite casually, listen, don't expect anything from the Casino … the Patricians said to me their coffers are in a meagre state, and you are not a virtuoso who could expect a golden sovereign." Mozart was furious, but still played two concertos and a trio on the violin. "I would have liked to have played the fiddle more, but I was so badly accompanied that it gave me the colic."

Adagio II: Medals and other Decorations

It was to get much worse – Leopold had given his son the well-meant tip to wear his Medal of the Golden Spur, awarded to him by Pope Clemens XIV in 1770, which should win the "regard and respect" of the "ruling king of diamonds", the Stadtpfleger Langenmantel. Or so he thought! But young Langenmantel, Jakob Alois Karl, thought he could have Mozart's papal medal copied for himself: "So, I will send to you tomorrow, and you will be good enough to lend me the cross for just a second, and I will send it back to you. Just so I can talk to the goldsmith… how much he values it at; so he will tell me about a Bavarian thaler. It isn't worth any more than that, since it isn't even gold but copper, ha ha." There was a confrontation. One word led to another. – Mozart: "I said, God forbid that it is made of tin, ha ha! I was burning with anger and rage." – Langenmantel jun.: "I can possibly leave out the spur?" – Mozart: "Oh yes, I said, you don't need one, you already have it in your head … he paled a little." Not without pathos, Mozart explained to the snotty young nobleman "von KurzenMantel" (short coat): "I can get all the medals that you can get before you could become what I am, even if you die twice and are reborn." Because of "such effrontery" Wolfgang decided to "let the whole patriciate lick his arse, and to leave". Only Bäsle prevented both, "if such a … dear Bäsle were not here, I would regret as much as I have hairs on my head that I ever came to Augsburg.

The old platitude about a prophet being honoured in his own country seemed to confirm itself in the case of Mozart. But despite the many troubles in the Langenmantel house, the piano maker Stein succeeded in bringing the deeply offended man round, and on October 16 there was indeed a concert "solely for the patricians" in the hall of the Herrentrinkstube opposite the Rathaus. Mozart played Piano Sonata K283. "Everything was good except for the accompaniment." Baron von Rehlingen thanked him kindly and gave him a risible 2 ducats, that is 10 gulden. For comparison, when the showman Martin Berschitz, who performed physical experiments in his booth, gave a guest performance to the Jesuits of St. Salvator in Augs-

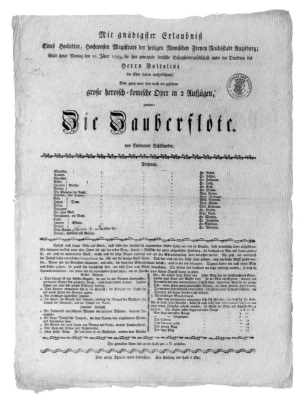

burg in 1779, he was paid 150 gulden. Mozart remembered the concert as "the high-class farmhouse academy". Who wouldn't liked to have been present at that memorable evening, about which Wolfgang reported to Salzburg "there were many noblesse there, the Duchess Arserumble, Count Pisswell and Princess Reeklikemuck, with her two daughters, but they are already married to the two princes Mustbelly von Sowsprick…"

But it remains a mystery how the untiring Stein then managed to wring a second concert out of Mozart for October 22, this time in public in the concert hall of the Fugger House. At any rate, the advertisement in the Augsburg Staats- und Gelehrtenzeitung makes a really big announcement: "Something for art and music lovers! Honour for us, dear patriot! To have a musician, a compatriot here, for whom we are the envy of the whole of England, France and Italy. Those who are a little familiar with political newspapers will know that it can be no other than Herr Chevalier Wolfgang Amadee Mozart, who in his tender youth performed so many miracles in the aforementioned nations. Let us see if he also does it for us?... Herr Mozart will do his best to entertain his gentle countrymen magnificently for several hours."

And that's what he did! The review appeared on October 24, and was a eulogy. Stein just happened to have completed three forte pianos, so that they could play a trio, Mozart, the cathedral organist, Johann Michael Demmler and Stein himself. Among the pieces they played was the Lodron Concerto (K242), Allegro, Adagio and Rondeau – "a powerful concerto for three pianos … Everything was extremely tasteful and admirable … The composition thorough, fiery, multifaceted and simple: the harmony so full, so forceful, so unexpected, so uplifting; the melody so pleasant, so balletic, and everything so new; the performance on the forte piano so nice, so pure, so full of expression, and at the same time so extraordinarily swift that one hardly knew what one should notice first, and all the audience were enthralled … The patriotically minded had the special pleasure of seeing, from the silence and the general applause of the audience, that we here know how to appreciate true beauty." To Mozart's greatest satisfaction, he was able to report to Salzburg: "the concert here turned

She, too, is Mozart: Gertrud Kottermaier aka "die Mozartin" at the Stein fortepiano in the Augsburg Mozart House.

out to be unsurpassed; the details are in the newspaper."

Rondeau: Farts and Prelate's Escalope

"The concert brought in 90 gulden without deduction of expenses. Now, with 2 ducats from the Stube we have taken 100 gulden. The expenses for the concert didn't amount to more than 16 gulden 30 kreuzer. I had the room for free ... So we have lost 26 or 27 gulden in all. It goes on." The continued journey assured, packing, a last visit to relations; on the morning of Sunday the 26th, departure from Augsburg. Except for two short stays later, never to set foot here again! What remained of Mozart in his Papa's home town? One thing is certain – In Jesuitengasse 26, a remorseful Bäsle and a volume of poetry probably moist with tears ("Votre tres affectioné Neveu Wolfgang Amadée Mozart") and, in silent expectation, ... a good dozen very coarse letters ("I shit on your nose", etc. etc.).

Mozart's Bäsle: Maria Anna Thekla Mozart was 18 $\frac{1}{2}$ years old in 1777, and spent her youth in Augsburg, where she bore an illegitimate daughter in 1784 (not by her cousin!), moved to Kaufbeuren, and to Bayreuth in 1814, where she died in 1841, a whole half-century after Wolfgang. Her cousin described her as "pretty, sensible, sweet, clever and comical" and "also a little bad". A little? From Leopold Mozart, we hear that his niece is said to have "too much familiarity with clerics". In fact when visiting St. Ulrich's, where they were received by Pater Aemilian Angermayr ("a courtly donkey and a simple joker in his profession"), Wolfgang noted, not without a trace of jealousy "He (Pater Aemilian) always wanted to have his sport with Bäsle, but she had her sport with him". Of course, he emphatically denied his father's charge that Bäsle was "no more than a 'Pfaffenschnitzel' (prelate's escalope) ... and she (Bäsle herself) protests solemnly against the Pfaffenschnitzel" Of course, Mozart senior, as so often, had to be right. As regards the originator of the above-mentioned illegitimate child – "a canon has made her happy". But what can have led Mozart father and son in 1777 to hand over manuscripts to the Augsburg Augustine Abbey of Heilig Kreuz for copying (now,

by the way, Augsburg's only truly historic Mozart holdings), rashly installing, of all people, "Bäsle" to supervise them? Let us hope that only critical copy editing took place behind the abbey walls ...

In his letters to his Bäsle, Mozart wrote many witty and even more stupid things, but very few really personal details. Nine have survived; at least two have been lost or subsequently destroyed, out of consideration for delicate public sensibilities. The last dates from October, 1781. That was already four years after Mozart's brief but passionate affair with Aloysia Weber from Mannheim, less than a year later he was to marry her sister Constanze. We can leave it to the reader's imagination what should be read between the lines, or may have been contained in Mozart's lost letter to "Mademoiselle Mariaenne", his "chèr Cousine", his "Bäsle bunny", his "très chére Niéce! Cousine! Fille! Mére, Sœur, et Epouse!", his "dearest, best, fairest, most lovable and charming little bass fiddle or violoncello infuriated by an unworthy cousin.

Since a concerned mother had probably scanned the letters to Bäsle in advance, the amorous correspondence, too, will not yield a satisfactory answer to those voyeuristic questions (what really happened in Augsburg – in Jesuitengasse or in silent organ lofts?). It speaks in favour of the accused and against such an act having taken place that, in December 1781, two months after the last letter to Bäsle, Wolfgang assured his father that, "therefore I can also swear that I have not had anything to do in that way with any female person..."

Letter us therefore keep our speculations to ourselves! Let us remember Joanne Chrisostomus Wolfgang Gottlieb Mozart as a genius who is above such profanities. Let us keep Augsburg in our memories as the German Mozart city, which held the lowest of the low, but also the highest of the high, for its great grandson. Finally, let us take our leave of Mozart, of Bäsle and the Mozart city of Augsburg as inimitably as only such a genius himself could do: "Now live well; I kiss you 10,000 times and remain as ever the old young sow's prick Wolfgang Amadé Rosenkranz."

Once upon a time, there was a man with a great love for the theatre. The man was an actor, like his wife, who supported him energetically in everything he did. In 1943, they built a small home stage together, the "puppet chest". The man was called Walter Oehmichen. With his wife and two daughters, he performed for friends of the family and they were delighted by the tiny marionette theatre, which gave a spark of light in dark times. The little theatre didn't survive the war, but the vision remained. In the three years following 1945, Walter and Rose Oehmichen created a new, larger, marionette stage, practically from nothing. Despite meagre resources and with great dedication – in the rooms of the Heilig-Geist-Spital by city architect Elias Holl – Oehmichen's dream became reality on February 26, 1948, when the lid of the chest opened for the first time.

Manfred Jenning was involved almost from the beginning. Still a young actor in 1948, Manfred's wide range of talents helped to shape and enrich the Puppenkiste. He gave his voice to a diverse array of characters on strings, is numerous productions, such as "Aladin", "Räuber Hotzenplotz" or for a long time the annual "cabaret programme" have made him unforgotten to this day; he was house poet, director and also producer for many TV productions (from 1960 to 1979).

Thanks to his good contacts, Walter Oehmichen and his Puppenkiste succeeded in being accepted by the Augsburg Association of Municipal Theatres. That still means more to the marionette theatre than just a recognition of his work (for example, the Augsburg Theatre provides a lighting technician with great

AUGSBURGER
PUPPENKISTE

experience of the stage). Oehmichen also designed a mobile version of his stage, so that the Augsburg team could now give guest performances in other cities.

The many TV productions (mostly in cooperation with the Hessischer Rundfunk) made the Puppenkiste's performances famous throughout Germany. The opening chest lid had become a symbol of lovingly created children's entertainment. "Die Muminfamilie" (1959), "Jim Knopf and Lukas der Lokomotivführer" (1961) and "Urmel aus dem Eis" (1969) were among the many Puppenkiste productions to enliven the German TV scene. Despite economic difficulties, the small stage became established over the years, not least thanks to the commitment of all the family members and the ensemble. Oehmichen's daughter Hannelore developed a great creative talent, and carved the figures for the new productions. It was also Hannelore who continued her father's inheritance – she took over direction in 1973 together with her husband Hanns-Joachim Marschall.

Walter Oehmichen died in 1977, and Manfred Jenning two years later. Rose Oehmichen followed them in 1985. They leave behind a reputable stage – created out of nothing and guided to great renown. The next generation is by no means resting on the founders' laurels. Theatre director Hanns-Joachim Marschall is guiding the Puppenkiste safely through choppy waters – in the 1980s, the city of Augsburg reduced its financial support, even though visitors' interest was continuing undiminished. It was not until 1991 that they found themselves on more solid ground again, after the city of Augsburg, the region of Swabia and the Free State of Bavaria had agreed on a rescue plan. The theatre direction is now in the hands of the third generation, the brothers Jürgen and Klaus Marschall. Under their leadership, the Puppenkiste had to manage a mammoth project in 1996: The filming of the story of "Monty Spinneratz" for the cinema screen. Two years later, there was another reason to celebrate – the Augsburger Puppenkiste was 50 years old. The jubilee was crowned with a huge German tour that lasted over two years. Another project in 2000 was the complete renovation of the dilapidated theatre, in

Left-hand side:
Sleeping Beauty (1989), Rumpelstiltskin (1998); Mozart on the trip to Prague (1956).

Right-hand side:
With the Angsthase in the clinic; in the "Die Kiste" puppet museum; the brothers Jürgen (left) and Klaus Marschall.

which the stage and auditorium were moved to the other side of the building, required patience and strong nerves by everyone involved. Nevertheless, they still found time to continue the TV story "Lilalu in Schepperland" shortly afterwards.

The Puppenkiste broke entirely new ground with its project "Das kleine Känguru und der Angsthase", which has run since spring 2003 with the support of the Hexal Foundation. Four puppeteers from the ensemble visit children's hospitals throughout Germany to perform a small piece to give encouragement to the children, whose sickness won't let them visit a puppet theatre so easily. A similar technique – with figures on short strings and in an open performance – is used for "Paula und den Kistenkobolden", an action that was launched with the cooperation of the Beta-institut. Since 2006, they have performed a small work to help kindergarten children understand their own feelings – with music to sing along to and four colourful goblins, who are respectively anxious, happy, angry or sad, and help the children to learn that that is all part of life.

Great sadness was caused by the death of "puppet mother" Hannelore in 2003. She left behind a wonderful and extraordinary inheritance in the almost 6,000 marionettes she created. However, she was still able to see the realization of her great dream – the creation and opening of the museum "Die Kiste" in the rooms above the theatre, which is sponsored by the association "Friends of the Augsburg Puppet Theatre", and where – besides circulating exhibitions with figures from all over the world – the Augsburg stars on strings, such as Urmel, Jim Knopf and Sams have found a fine home.

Now, the son Jürgen Marschall, as head of the puppet workshop, is continuing his mother's legacy well into the future. He is now creator of the much-loved little wooden-heads, who delight children and grown ups alike with their charm – whenever they open the chest lid, almost every day.

The founders, Walter and Rose Oehmichen, would still have great joy in their good old, new, little, big puppet chest, which celebrates its 60th birthday in 2008.

The whole city is one big park. And everyone has his own personal space – somewhere on the water, perhaps or in the splendid Hofgarten.

FAVOURITE PLACES

Favourite Places

The view is most striking from the air. Seen from above, Bavaria's third-biggest city looks as though the houses and factories, roads and railway lines have impertinently eaten their way into a green jungle – and are now merely tolerated. No wonder. The whole city is one big park. There are good reasons why Augsburg is one of the few German metropolises with an above-average share of green spaces – two thirds of the city is undeveloped, and has just been left to nature. At the "green city competition" in 1997, Augsburg was widely praised as the "greenest city with the highest quality of life" and even won a European gold medal. And every Augsburger has his favourite place in one of the green spots, in Siebentischwald, in a secluded corner of the Botanical Garden or on a concealed bench by the river Wertach.

Favourite places. They are oases of calm, of silence, of relaxation. Places that make you feel good. Where you meet friends, read a book, let yourself go. Somewhere, out there. It's only a short trip, just a few steps, a few minutes by bike into the greenery near your flat. Sometimes you only need to look around the corner, where a few trees, a meadow, a handful of benches are gathered between the houses. If you want recreation, it's never far away in Augsburg – whether you live in the inner city or in one of the districts. And almost every quarter has an adjacent woodland, meadow or parkscape; there's plenty of opportunity for recreation.

The Hofgarten is such a favourite place. Amidst the noisy city, amidst life, the small park is a place for beach mats and holding hands, for newspaper reading and a midday nap. A piece of Italy in Augsburg. Behind artistic iron railings, the lovingly created garden of the former prince-episcopal residence, surrounded by magnificent historic buildings, where the government of Swabia now resides. Created between 1739 and 1744 by the baroque master architect Johann Caspar Bagnato, this jewel has been open to the public since 1965. Where once the bishops strolled, fruit was cultivated after the Second World War. Now hibiscus bushes and Chinese wisteria, tulip and ginkgo trees thrive here between white park benches and obscure sandstone gnome figures. The box trees have been trimmed into conical forms; the roses bloom in all the colours of summer. A fountain splashes away, ornamental fish and European turtles play in the water lily pond. The Hofgarten is a solarium, terrace and reading room for hundreds of inner city dwellers. This three-metre-high mahogany book case has been available here in the north-east corner of the park since 2001. The open-air library displays "Brehm's Animal Life" alongside "The Temptation of Angelique", the Brigitte recipe book besides Goethe's "Italian journey". Anyone can help himself and anyone can leave books here.

It is only a few steps from the Hofgarten to Fronhof. In the great 1.4 hectare park in the shadow of the high cathedral and the prince bishop's residence, full of exotic and native flowers and old trees, there is always a place in the sun on the meadow. It is there to be used, to be crowded, to be lived in. Tourists lie on the grass and browse through their guide books, school classes eat lunch, civil servants from the municipal offices take their lunch break here.

These green oases make the city such a wonderful place to live in, which is why they are so important to the Augsburgers. They lovingly tend the natural, enchantingly beautiful corners of their city. The city greenery even flourishes along the streets. The balconies are often wildly overgrown, sunflowers even flourish on the fourth floor and even the smallest windowsill has space for a pot of herbs. It seems almost natural that the first tulip in Europe speared its way out of the ground in an Augsburg garden. The patrician Johannes Heinrich Herwart had gained wealth and fame in commerce and apparently allowed himself the luxury of a botanical garden with unusual flowers and plants. Reverentially and with a respect for his city, he gave the name "Semper Augustus" to his tulip, which bloomed in his Renaissance garden in April 1559.

Augsburg is still a city of gardeners – mainly allotment holders. On average there is 8.6 square metres of allotment space for every resident. Almost every district has a huge allotment area neatly fenced up into parcels, with garden gnomes keeping watch and Bavarian flags flying, with meticulously cut lawns, luxuriant flower beds and its own beer garden. Very private favourite places. And those without a garden can get their own fresh kitchen herbs in the herb garden at Rabenbad in the city wall parks – picking is expressly permitted. Framed by low box hedges, Spanish, Russian, Roman and grandma's mint, dill, lovage, sage, fennel and thyme grow in large beds according to a historic model. A playground as a stop for the little ones is not far away – one of 180 distributed through the city area. As well as 54 playing fields. A good 50 hectares for just playing, romping around and building sandcastles.

Narrow footpaths lead to small, neatly kept gardens along the moat, crossing the stream and canal network of the city of three rivers at a host of catwalks and bridges – far more bridges than in Venice, by the way. Over 500

There are many favourite places for relaxing and dreaming. At Kuhsee, for example, at Kahnfahrt, at Hochablass, where water has been diverted and fed through the canals and city streams for centuries.

Water and wood-
land draw us
magically. In
Augsburg, it is
never far to the
greenery near
your flat or the
romantically lush
meadows of the
Wertach and Lech.

have been counted in Augsburg, across the Lech, Wertach and Singold. In 1462, Emperor Friedrich III gave the Augsburgers the right to divert as many streams as necessary from the Lech – so vital were the canals for transport and trade: for the tanners, dyers and furriers. Now, the quietly murmuring streams and canals are favourite places of many residents of the old city.

At Rotes Tor, open-air stages plays were performed at the wall gardens as early as 1929. The tradition has been preserved to this day. Since 1932 – interrupted only by the Second World War – the Augsburg Theatre ensemble has performed in summer at the 2,117-seater open-air theatre, the biggest in South Germany.

Here, in the park gardens "at the walls and moats" created in the 19th century at the express wish of the citizens, Nature is left to its own devices. Here, on a balmy moonlit night, Anne and Tom carved a heart and arrow into the parkbench, bumblebees buzz here over the rampant weeds, the city residents walk their dogs – along the old ruins of the former city walls, past towers and defence trenches. It was in the mid-fifteenth century, when Augsburg replaced the former palisade fence by a city wall. The fortifications are now a broad, green belt. It astonishes every stranger driving along the tree-lined alleys for the first time – showing how incomparably green this city is. In Augsburg, even places surrounded by raging traffic, like Königsplatz, are verdant. The roads and squares with fountains at the central nodes of the bus and tram network were created in 1860 following a baroque example.

There's one quiet spot that is a favourite of many Augsburgers: the Kahnfahrt (boating lake) at the city moat. Even Bertolt Brecht – raised within view of it – is said to have sat reading and musing for hours on the iron railings around the moat. In 1876, the Augsburger Paul Kurz started not only a family, but also the boat hire business. Since then, this charming and idyllic beer garden, surrounded by shady old chestnuts has been a family owned business – now in the fourth generation. A green island directly on the water. On the day of its foundation, Paul Kurz, almost certainly with his young bride

Babette, rowed over the gurgling water in one of the three boats he built himself.

The bastion Lueginsland is similarly history laden. Like the walls and moats, it is a remnant of the days when the Imperial City had to be defended with walls, towers and gates. The road to the northern fortified wall of the old city leads up via overgrown stairs, past crumbling city walls and ancient trees. At a favourite place where – in probably Augsburg's finest city beer garden – you are also well supplied with food and drink. By the way, with a lot of imagination, you have a wonderful view across the city, over the northern Lech valley and Wolfzahnau.

The Lech and Wertach rivers flow together here, water and woodland. A broad strip of park follows the two rivers through the city – a wide space to enjoy Nature. A paradise for joggers, strollers and cyclists. The city fathers can be thanked for that, who had to plan the reconstruction after the war. A great deal of rubble was dumped on the riverbanks. But, over the debris of war there grew up sweeping meadows with playing fields and tobogganing slopes, with meadows, avenues and footpaths. For those who need a rest, there are any number of beer gardens along the Wertach. Small and big, new and old established, like the Kulperhütte, not far from Rosenau stadium. It has been here – picturesquely situated between the Wertach and Wertach canal – for 80 years. With deckchairs along a sort of city beach, it has become the in place to meet. The beer garden in Wellenburg is similarly frequented – probably because a wonderful romantic avenue with over 200 old lime trees leads there.

Locations like the Kulperhütte, which attract young Augsburgers now, had their equivalent before the War in the magnificent city gardens for the culturally-minded and self-aware citizenry. They met there, chatted over coffee and cake, spent their Sundays there and admired the rose borders and flower beds in the changing seasons. An attractive little pavilion has remained from the glory days of the city garden by the current Congress Hall, a few flowers shrubs, trees and a pond. But the former magnificence has faded; of the city garden, all that remains is a boring lawn as a backdrop for the "corn

The desire for greenery makes the city such a good place to live, as here at Jakobertor.

cobs". The unusually tower block, spiralling 35 storeys into the sky, is known locally as the highest lookout point in Augsburg.

Most residents of the area are drawn to the nearby Wittelsbacher Park, which, at almost 21 hectares, is the largest green space in the built-up city area. The park, with its extensive meadows, footpaths and sturdy park trees, was only called after the Wittelsbacher royal family in 1906, but the forerunners of the park had already existed for a long time. Until the trade fair centre was built, the Augsburger Frühjahrsausstellung (spring exhibition) was held here once a year. Now it is mainly a meeting point for mums pushing prams, pensioners taking a walk, and kids playing football.

The Augsburgers have always been driven by this desire for the greenery that makes the

city so natural. In the 19th century, the citizens demanded an idyllic route out to the countryside beyond the southern city gates. They called on Carl von Effner, the royal court garden director, who had created the Englischer Garten in Munich. The Augsburgers liked him so much that they asked the highly regarded landscape architect to link their city walls to the Stadtwald (city wood). And so – like a green network – Siebentisch park was created. The 30-hectare Siebentisch gardens connect with over 2,000 hectares of city woodland.

Close nearby are the Zoo and Botanical Garden – two green spots that have joined up with Siebentisch park to form an outsized leisure complex in the middle of the city. In 1936, the small city garden plant nursery became a modest teaching and show garden. Then, during the garden exhibition in 1985,

its area was doubled to ten hectares, smartened up and modernised. Today, the Botanical Garden is a favourite place equally for those seeking peace and quiet, flower lovers and music fans. A flourishing lime-tree avenue, flocks of twittering birds, and butterflies flapping in formation welcome the visitors in summer. Some 1,200 different shrubs, wild herbs, grasses and ferns take root here, more than a million bulbous plant take turns to bloom. Every tree, every shrub, every copse bears a label. Gardening in orderly proportions – the tropical plants live under glass in the hothouses; tomatoes and chives grow in the farm garden, and medicinal herbs grow in the apothecary garden. The Botanical Garden is a place to feel good – a pyrotechnic display of scents and colours. In the rose and music garden alone, 3,600 cultivated roses in almost 60 different sorts lap around concrete terraces. On warm summer evenings – when the Botanical Garden is magically and mysteriously illuminated – the pavilion at its centre becomes a huge concert stage. The guests sit on the steps, twined around by roses in soft pink, shrill yellow, garish red, flattering white and surrounded by the seductively gentle scent of lavender. There is no more beautiful – or intensive – place to enjoy music.

Then, the Japanese garden is truly peaceful. Just a few steps further, where the strictly ordered Botanical Garden meets the Siebentisch Park, laid out in English chic, the magical 4,200 square-metre pond garden was created in 1984. It is regarded as one of the most important Japanese garden creations in Europe, indeed one of the finest outside Japan. The models for this playful dream of stone, water and wood can be found in the old Japanese imperial city of Kyoto. Swabian gardeners and Japanese horticulturists worked together on the second Bavarian Garden Exhibition – creating this magnificent tea garden, with pavilions, rocks, stone lanterns, dwarf pines, waterfall stones and wooden terraces as a living monument for the two Japanese twin cities of Amagasaki and Nagahama. A place of silence, sensuality and meditation.

The place next door is home grown. When it is time to feed the elephants and zebras, lions and seals, giraffes and meerkats, there's little time to rest in the Augsburg Zoo. There is a massive onslaught of mother-child groups and invasion of wooden carts, particularly in good weather. The favourite places for the youngest residents of Augsburg are with their animal friends. More than half a million visitors per year pass through the 22-hectare park, pervaded by natural watercourses and shaded by old trees – one of the biggest zoos in Southern Germany, by the way. The zoological garden was opened in 1937 as a "park of the German animal world", and populated with exotic animals as well after the Second World War. Today, it holds more than 1,500 animals of around 300 different kinds. And in the centre is the historic Goggelesbrücke (bridge) – a precious part of Augsburg. The wooden bridge was built in 1922 on the weir spanning the Wertach. It formed the transition to the Wertach suburban town and the city district of Pfersee – and the Augsburgers grew truly fond of the wooden structure. When it threatened to fall in 2005, a dramatic rescue venture was put into action. It was successful. Now, the old Goggelesbrücke stands in the Zoo, as a visitors' platform and shelter in the new seal enclosure.

The Zoo, Botanical Garden and Siebentischwald finally merge into the city wood, the most important green lungs of the city. That is where the drinking water for the metropolis comes from – and has done for centuries. It is drawn from protected wells, whose catchment areas are fenced around. The smooth juxtaposition of ecology and recreation makes the Augsburg city wood special throughout Europe. The way that the requirements of nature conservancy have been reconciled with human leisure needs has even impressed experts, and has gone down in the annals as the "Augsburg model". The city wood is of course also a treasure trove for favourite places. Woods, meadows, streams and kilometre after kilometre of hiking, cycling and riding paths have made it Augsburg's preferred recreational area – and the city into the biggest municipal woodland owner in the Bavaria, indeed the third biggest in Germany. The widely used, extensive woodland and unspoilt moorland, with rare plants and animals, is one of the biggest non-alpine nature conservancy areas in

A magnificent pavilion and a small pond remain from the heyday of the Augsburg city garden. From the time when the self-confident citizenry spent their Sundays in the park.

The Botanical Garden is a place to feel good. It issues a pyrotechnic display of scents and colours. The Japanese garden was created in 1984 as a living monument for the two Japanese twin towns of Amagasaki and Nagahama.

Bavaria. The beeches, maple and lime trees, or the bank of the Stempflesee (lake) are wonderful places to picnic, stroll around and switch off. And you always feel that the Augsburg conurbation is far away.

The paths of the Stadtwald landscape park stretch as far south as Lech barrage 23. Massive barrages continually interrupt the river, as it flows – sometimes turbulent and sometimes sluggish – towards the city. At the eastern edge of the Stadtwald, surrounded by the riverside woods and the Lech, is Kuhsee. It is Augsburg's chic leisure paradise par excellence. The lake, which was created in 1972, is particularly romantic in the early dawn. When only a solitary Nordic walker is doing his rounds, or a dog owner walking his four-legged friend. The "Qsee Café" is closed at this time, the broad gravel beach deserted, the climbing frame on the playground forlorn. On a fine day, though, there is hardly space to lay another towel, here; people bring cool bags and folding chairs; squadrons of frisbees fly through the air. The Kuhsee feels almost like Rimini. There's a place for everyone here – for the ice skaters and curlers in winter, and in summer for the anglers, swimmers and sun worshippers, divers, paddlers and raft builders.

A few metres on, on the gravel banks in the Lech, directly at Hochablass, lamb chops sizzle alongside bratwurst; the beer crates float in the Lech alongside the wine bottles, to keep cool. Here, on the Lech meadows and at the Kuhsee, people meet with friends on warm summer evenings, to grill, eat, and celebrate. The Lech splits at Hochablass, which, in summer, is pervaded by the scent of glowing charcoal, by the scent of freedom. The water supply with weir on the rushing Lech was created in the early middle ages. For centuries, water has been diverted at Hochablass and fed through the canals and city streams to provide power for the artisans in the old city. And the water for the ice canal in Hochzoll, Augsburg's Olympic canoe slalom. The canal was built in 1972 for the 20th Olympic summer games and at the time was the world's first artificial white-water course – 660 metres of surging water, given the character of white water by the concrete rocks. Today, it is a Federal German high-performance canoe training centre.

And if you still haven't found your favourite place in the city – no problem! Not only the city green spaces, but the great forest is also not far away. The city lies at the edge of the extensive nature park Augsburg Westliche Wälder, a 117,500 hectare recreational area between the rivers Wertach, Schmutter, Mindel and Danube. Even more space, then, for cycling, walking, feeling good and for recreation.

Recreation and sport far from the coast – everything is possible in Augsburg or a canoe slalom through the ice canal.

46 Wertachbruckertor (Wertach Bridge Gate). The city gate was built in 1370 on a bridge with customs office over the Wertach. The gate was reconstructed in 1605 by the city architect Elias Holl.

47 Fischertor (Fisher Gate). The modern two-storey gate is a Neobaroque building from 1924/25. Fischertor connects with the old ring wall.

48 Hexenbrunnen (Witch Fountain). A Venetian wall fountain is located in a wall niche at the base of Schwedenstiege (steps). The steep steps lead down to the city moat.

49 Oblatter Wall. The earth wall was created in 1540 as a circular bastion with a strong fortified tower at the city side. Entrance to the Augsburger Kahnfahrt (boating lake), with boat hire from April to October.

50 Fünfgratturm (Five-Ridge Tower). A tower built in 1455 with five turrets and a high tented roof. Now free standing, the tower was formerly integrated into the eastern city wall.

51 Jakobertor (St. James' Gate). Gothic gate tower with pointed gate arch build in the mid-15th century. The tower is preserved in its original form with remains of the city wall.

52 Vogeltor (Bird Gate). Built in 1445 as an outer gate of the city wall; partly burnt out in the bombing in 1944, it was rebuilt in 1954.

53 Rotes Tor (Red Gate). The most important outer gate in the south of the city, through which the trading route to Tyrol and Italy passed. Redesigned by Elias Holl in 1622.

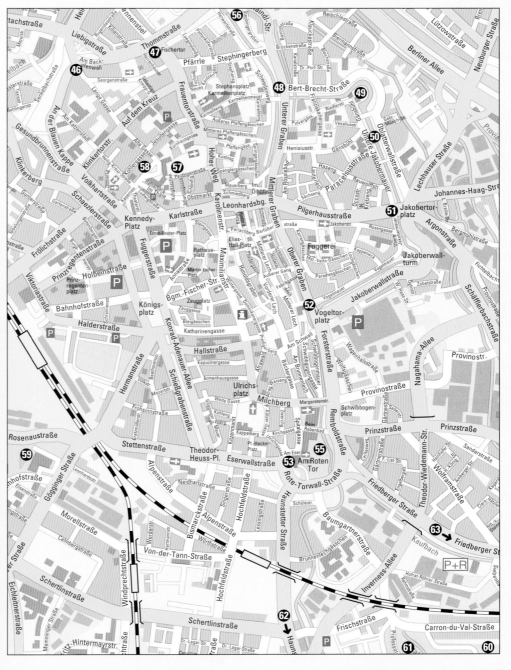

Bavaria and mountains belong together, at least in the tourist publicity. No wonder, then, that visitors from the north, east or west of Germany are surprised when they approach Augsburg for the first time. Where are the alpine peaks, glistening with snow even in summer? Many had not imagined that the landscape around the South Bavarian metropolis would be so flat.

Only when the warm southerly down-wind, the Föhn, blows does the mountain silhouette seem close enough to touch. And the Zugspitze seems to loom up next to the hotel tower – the illusion even fascinates the locals every time, despite the headaches that many suffer from the Föhn. Those who come frequently stay for a long time, or even put down roots in Augsburg, and quickly forget their initial disappointment about the 100-kilometre distance to the alpine foothills. On the Lech plane it is easier to cycle than in the mountains, and it is not so strenuous if you want to investigate the small hillocks to the left and right.

The "Augsburg Westliche Wälder" nature park with the rustic cultural landscape of the "Stauden" at Fischach in the south-west and the wooded corner in the north-west is a recreation area on your doorstep. That is where the Mozart family came from; where the Fuggers increased their possessions and influence, and where the famous local author Ludwig Ganghofer spent his childhood. East of the Lech, in the hills of the Tertiary period, the "Wittelsbacher Land" tempts you to discover old-Bavarian culture and to bathe in the many lakes. Testaments to Bavarian popular piety can be seen in every direction. Pilgrimage churches and monasteries, where traditionally you can also enjoy a small meal, are recommended for self reflection and as architectural attractions. Leisure parks, such as Fred Rai's Western City or the indoor playground "Jimmy's Fun Park" in Dasing, the woodland rope park "Robin's Wood" in Rehling-Scherneck and the all-season swimming paradises of "Königstherme" in Königsbrunn and "Titania" in Neusäß also provide diversion for children.

The Augsburger can feel at home in the Westliche Wälder. Here, everything is available for day trippers from the city. An exten-

sive network of well-marked footpaths and cycle-touring routes leads you through the forests and fields. For tired walkers and cyclists, there are benches to rest on; idyllic nooks are signposted. If you leave the city on route 300 towards Memmingen, you can enjoy a foretaste of the recreational landscape just past the city limits. At Steppach, the Bismarck Tower on Sandberg – an angular stone monument erected at the beginning of the 20th century at the edge of a small park – is a popular gathering place on Sunday mornings for a chat and to relax your tense muscles. It is going too far to call this modest hill a vantage point, but from here you gain a good impression of how the city has spread.

AROUND AUGSBURG

But we want to leave the city behind us and breathe country air. One possible starting point is Anhausen, a district of Diedorf. After a detour into the homely church of St. Adelgundis, built by the baroque architect Hans Georg Mozart, a great uncle of the eminent composer Wolfgang Amadeus, an inconspicuous sign leads out to the Anhauser Tal (valley). Here, where the tarred road ends and car drivers must leave their vehicles at a small parking lot in the woods, is the start of the sanctuary for pedestrians and cyclists. The Anhauser stream meanders through the fields and pastures of the valley, which opens in a southerly direction. Light and warmth course pleasantly through body and soul; there is a good feeling. A Pfisterer family erected a roadside cross here in 2003, asking "God's blessing for our lands and protection on our journeys." Just off the path, spring water splashes in a hollow tree trunk – "Weber's Brünnele" (fountain) is the name of this lovingly designed rest stop. Though there is little peace for those who like to be alone. There are a lot of people around; Anhauser Tal is not only famous because golf ace Bernhard Langer has his home here.

The next destination to the south-west could be Oberschönenfeld. The Cistercian convent in the Schwarzach valley, near Gessertshausen, founded in the 13th century, is at the heart of the nature park, even though the secluded area of the convent remains out of bounds to visitors. Attractions here, besides the baroque church and restaurant, are the outhouses of the former convent estate. They include the folklore museum of the region of Swabia with a permanent exhibition about country life, and a collection of agricultural implements and rotating exhibitions about culture and contemporary art in Swabia. Door to door with the convent bakery, where the nuns bake and sell their fragrant bread, is the nature park house, giving a view into the mysteries of the wood.

The tour of discovery continues along the rivers Schmutter and Neufnach, down to the "Stauden" in the region of Unterallgäu. It is only relatively recently that the cities learnt to appreciate the advantages of this compact cultural landscape, subdivided by hedges and farm tracks. This area used to be considered poor and backward; now many day trippers are delighted to rediscover unspoilt nature, thought to have disappeared.

On the Stauden meditation road, from Fischach you can feel the effect of the landscape or, if interested in culture, take a walk north to Weiler Heimberg, where Mozart's forefathers were ploughing fields and milking cows as early as the 15th century. Not far away is Buschelberg, which has been a fortified retreat since the Neolithic age. That is indicated by ceramic finds.

The community of Fischach was also something of a refuge for the Jews from the 16th century. While they were persecuted elsewhere, here – against payment of protection money – they were at least tolerated in Fischach under the Habsburg sovereigns of the time. We are reminded of the once flourishing Jewish life – extinguished in the Third Reich – by weathered gravestones behind the locked gate of the Jewish cemetery on Kohlberg.

The northern edge of the Westliche Wälder nature park is almost an insider tip, but the drive on route 2, past the radar complex at Gablingen and several industrial and commercial areas gives no indication of the fabu-

A recreational landscape is provided by the Westliche Wälder and Stauden. Its "heart" is the Kloster Oberschönenfeld convent (previous page) with the folklore museum.

lous nooks to be found there. It is still almost 40 kilometres from the centre of Augsburg to the monastery Kloster Holzen (district of Allmannshofen). It is particularly charming to approach on a minor road, via Gut Schwaighof near Nordendorf. Grazing horses and cattle lift their heads in interest when a car occasionally passes. With luck, a crowing cock can even be heard here in the country-side on the road to Hahnenweiler. On the sunny bank of the Schmutter, free-range ducks dry their feathers after a dip in the river. In the shadow of high trees, the hiking route "Rund um die Klause" leads to the monastery with its fine, stylishly decorated restaurant. On foot, you walk uphill over a steep stairs, past a dilapidated house and a silent graveyard to a clearing. By car, you come from the south west on the official access road.

Refugees from the city can breathe deeply here and take their time. The sundial on the inside of the northern monastery gatehouse is in any case an hour late from the end of March until October. John the Baptist, his staff serving as a clock hand, still orients himself to the natural position of the sun and is therefore usually "running late". He is excused by the years 1710–1927 over the sweeping baroque arch – they didn't know about "daylight saving" in those days.

The Benedictine Abbey of Holzen was secularized in 1802. For more than a century, the monastery estates belonged to the noble family von Fischler-Treuberg, until they were transferred to the possession of St. Josef's congregation of Ursberg in 1927. Since then, handicapped persons have lived and worked here. But there are moments when the monastic spirit comes alive again. On this Wednesday afternoon, cheerful female voices sound through the open windows of the church gallery, which once belonged to the secluded area of the monastery. First they laugh, then sing. Songs of praise fill the clear church room with the rich white Wessobrunn stucco, which cheers you up, taking the terror out of the reliquary shrines with their skulls in the side altars.

The chubby-cheeked Christ child in his glass shrine is somewhat more consoling. It came to Holzen in 1647; in 1713, it healed a possessed woman from Krumbach and since then has been venerated as a helper in need. It has answered the prayers of the devout until the present day – "the little Jesus of Holzen helped", can be seen on a candle bearing the year 1996.

Like Kloster Holzen, the pilgrimage churches of St. Jakobus, St. Laurentius and zum Heiligen Kreuz in Biberbach lie on one of the pilgrimage roads to Santiago de Compostela. This is the next station for the pilgrims following this route from Ries. The miraculous image above the high altar, a late-Romanesque crucifix, is famous – though under the wrong name. As the "Herrgöttle von Biberach" (Lord God of Biberach) it is often mistakenly assigned to Biberach an der Riss in Upper Swabia. But there is no doubt that the "dear little Lord God", to which many hundreds of answered prayers were ascribed between 1681 and 1761, lives here, in this magnificent rococo church of Biberbach. Apart from during church services and on guided tours (every Sunday and Friday at 3:00 pm), visitors are only permitted to see into the altar room through a wrought-iron grating.

The church with the ornate onion-dome towers is historically interesting for yet another reason – On November 6, 1766, the ten-year-old Wolfgang Amadeus Mozart matched himself here against another musical Wunderkind, the twelve-year-old Joseph Siegmund Eugen Bachmann. "Everyone did his best to deny the other the advantage, and the competition turned out very honourable for both", reported the "Musical Correspondent of the German Philharmonic Society" in 1790. Without this newspaper report, the episode would probably have been forgotten, since Leopold Mozart, the ambitious father of Wolfgang Amadé – probably ashamed that his son did not clearly win the day – devoted not a word to it in his diary.

When making church and monastery tours in the North of Augsburg, it is worth making a detour to Thierhaupten on the east side of the Lech. The foundation of the Benedictine monastery by Duke Tassilo III in the eighth century has become surrounded with many legends. In one version, depicted on a fresco in the former monastery church, the Duke had lost his way in the woods during a hunt.

The Kloster Holzen monastery (bottom) provides a place for the handicapped to live and work. The former monastery of Thierhaupten (below right) also includes the mill (right), which is now a monument to technology and a museum.

The famous "liabe Herrgöttle von Biberach" ("dear Lord god of Biberach"), a miracle-working crucifix, can be found in the pilgrimage church in Biberbach nother of Augsburg.

A hind led him back to his hunting party, whereupon he founded the monastery in thanks. The monastery ensemble on a hill at the south eastern border is impressive mainly for its massive dimensions. In 1983, the market town purchased the desolate complex of buildings, which had passed through several hands since its secularisation. The huge feat of renovating it was accomplished in partnership with the region of Swabia, the municipal urban development department, the rural district of Augsburg and the department for the preservation of historic buildings. The continuation of the estate is secured by public use. While signposts at the Thierhaupten entrance arouse great expectations about the monastery mill museum, this, too, must be visited at the right time – from May to October, on Sundays and holidays from 2 to 5 pm and by arrangement. Thanks to great dedication by private individuals, the historic mill has been thoroughly renovated and after some years as a private concern was presented to the rural district as a gift. Now, the object shares the fate of many museums outside tourist centres – it deserves far more attention.

All the destinations described so far lie in the rural district of Augsburg, including Thierhaupten, which is already in the Bavarian dialect region. Along the Lechrain to the south, it is not far from here to the "Wittelsbacher Land" – former enemy territory of the Augsburgers. It was only after opposition that parts of the present rural district of Aichach-Friedberg would allow themselves to be taken over by the Swabians in the regional reorganisation of 1972. Friedberg was a frontier fortification of the Wittelsbachers, who ruled Bavaria for more than 700 years. The city, founded in 1257, looks down on Lechtal from on high. If you want to discover the charming old town with the fine town houses behind the city wall, and the Renaissance castle with the attractive city museum, you have to go uphill from Augsburg. In the past, with coaches and horsedrawn carts, that was very laborious. But the very steep Friedberger Berg has now been tamed, and the destructions of the pillaging Augsburgers over the course of history have been pardoned. Since 1806, Augsburg has also been part of Bavaria. The former customs station between the territories is only remembered in the name of the district of Hochzoll, which has grown together with Friedberg-West below in the plane.

Where Augsburg stops and Friedberg begins can only be seen at the foot of the hill by the town signs – and by the Maria Alber chapel at the edge of route B 300. It is thus something of an outpost for other fine church buildings in the old Bavarian neighbourhood of the city of Augsburg, including the rococo pilgrimage church Herrgottsruh, with a nave and aisles, at the eastern edge of the old town of Friedberg. Famous names are connected to the history of this impressive house of God. The ceiling fresco in the choir cupola is a late work by Cosmas Damian Asam of 1738, the nave and aisles were decorated in 1749 by the great fresco painter Matthäus Günther and much of the stucco work is by Franz Xaver and Johann Michael Feichtmayr. The city parish church of St. Jakob in the centre is very different: The banded campanile with pointed roof was only created in the 19th century on a Veronese model, following a fire, and brings Italian flair to the city on the Romantic Road.

Kissing, Mering and Merching round off the trip to the countryside around Augsburg, from Friedberg southwards. On the way there, between Ottmaring and Kissing, lies Gut Mergenthau. In an evocatively designed museum, we can learn about "Hiasl of Bavaria" Matthäus Klostermayr (May to October, Saturday 2:00–7:00 pm and Sunday 1:00–7:00 pm). As a young lad, the poacher and robber chief was a hunting helper to the Jesuits. He lost his job for making fun of a father, who had shot a cat instead of a hare. Rebellious by nature, he wouldn't back down but rebelled against authority, became a folk hero and had to flee across the Lech into Swabia. As "Bayerischer Hiasl", he gained an infamous name for himself and his band. But it couldn't last forever. He was executed in 1771 in Dillingen when only 35 years old.

Klostermayr's birth town of Kissing grew at whirlwind pace into an "economic miracle" village after the Second World War. Seen from route 2, the modern part of the district doesn't look so enticing. But you will miss something if you just drive through – namely, the Burgstall chapel at the edge of the old town towards Ried. There is something curi-

The pilgrimage churches "Herrgottsruh" in Friedberg (left page) and "Maria Birnbaum" near Sielenbach (below right) are worthwhile goals in old Bavaria. Right, a view of the Friedberg city museum in the castle.

ous about the square, on which the baroque pilgrim church "Zur schmerzhaften Muttergottes" (for the suffering Mother of God) was built in 1681. It stands proud on a low hill, above the Lechfeld. Vertigo sufferers may have to pluck up courage before ascending the open flight of 61 steps. But it is worthwhile, even if the church door is closed for security reasons. If there really are places of spiritual energy with special vibrations, then this is one of them. It feels good to linger here, and the excellent view far out into Lechfeld, where the famous battle against the Hungarians raged somewhere between Kissing and Mering in 955, is not the only reason.

The historical importance of this ancient settlement area is attested to by archaeological finds in the Mering city museum. But life can be wonderful here nowadays, too. The centre of the market community, with its provincial feeling, conveys a feel-good atmosphere. This relaxed mood continues on the way back towards the Lech – Half way to Königsbrunn, at Lech barrier 23, the "Mandichosee" (lake), a paradise for bathers and surfers, has been created as a by-product of hydraulic power utilization. Downstream at the Kissing boundary, the idyllic Weitmannsee lies somewhat more hidden in a green belt resembling a riverside wood. This is a former gravel pit, where it is wonderful to lounge in summer and observe nature in the other seasons. Numerous types of water bird live here and breed on the many islands.

And if you want to penetrate further into the old-Bavarian countryside, the pilgrimage church of Maria Birnbaum, near Sielenbach, in Ecknachtal, north of the Stuttgart–Munich autobahn, is to be recommended. The Teutonic commander Philipp Jakob von Kaltenthal had it built from 1661 to 1668 to his personal concept, as a frame for a miracle-working Pietà who stood in a hollow pear tree. It is the first domed church on an Italian model created north of the Alps, richly ornamented with Wessobrunn stucco by the master Matthias Schmuzer. It is only a stone's throw from Maria Birnbaum to the chief town of Aichach and to Oberwittelsbach, where the ancestral castle of the Wittelsbachers stood until 1100. But that would be a chapter of its own.

Hard Times

Standing at my writing desk
I see through the window, in the garden, the elder bush
And in it identify some red and some black
And suddenly remember the elder
Of my childhood in Augsburg.
For some minutes I quite seriously
Consider going to the table
And fetching my spectacles to see
The black berries on the red twigs once more.
(Bertolt Brecht, 1955)

BERTOLT BRECHT

Bertolt Brecht, indisputably one of the greatest German-language authors of the 20th century, came into the world on 10th February 1898 at an insignificant place – in a small workman's house in Augsburg's old city. The address now is Auf dem Rain 7. At the time Brecht was born, the ground floor was occupied by a file factory, its hammers driven by one of the Lech canals that flowed around the house. Brecht's father, later a respected director of the Haindl paper factory, was already an employee with this company. With his wife, he had to share the apartment in the first floor of the house with two clothing traders. A few months after Bertolt was born, the family moved to the more sizable house nearby at "Bei den sieben Kindeln No. 1", where Bertolt's brother Walter was born in 1900.

By far the greatest part of Brecht's childhood, which he recalls in the famous poem *Hard Times,* was spent in the Haindl company-owned house in Bleichstraße 2, where the family had a generously sized apartment from September 12, 1900 – the father had become a purchaser with the paper factory and administered the four Haindl foundation houses. Thus, when still only twelve, Brecht had two attic rooms to himself from 1910, which could be reached from a separate entrance. The attic was later to become one of

the most important meeting places of the young poet's circle of friends – the starting point and scene of many of the clique's activities, but also where some early poetic works were created. Thus, bourgeois values prevailed for the Brechts during these years, and they were very conscious of the family's social standing.

As modest as the house is, so Brecht's literary beginnings are similarly unspectacular. The earliest surviving literary document is the so-called *Diary No. 10,* which reports on the time from June to December 1913, and besides biographical entries also contains a series of poetic efforts. It shows a fifteen-year-old who was inspired by his desire to become a famous author, a goal to which everything else seemed subordinated. He submitted his first contributions to newspapers for publication – naturally without success. For the first time, a characteristic emerged that was to remain typical of Brecht for the rest of his life: He didn't give up, but continued to pursue his great goal doggedly: if no one wanted to print his text, he created his own medium for it; the student newspaper *Die Ernte* (The Harvest) emerged, called into being and published by him.

Brecht's literary contributions to newspapers and his diary show that a highly com-

mitted, but by no means strikingly talented, student is at work here; he knows all too well that his plans to become established as a poet can only come to fruition if he is prepared from the start to acquire the necessary craftsmanship through determined hard work. His first contributions are thus primarily sober attempts to imitate all possible literary genres and authors. He also acquired a comprehensive knowledge of world literature, which he practically soaked up. Another striking characteristic of Brecht emerges in context with the little newspaper project, and once again it is a matter of sober rationality. To maintain the newspaper over several editions, he needed sufficient texts from his fellow students, but they were not available in the necessary quantities. So Brecht gave his own texts to the others, for publication under their names. In this way, they were able

to advancing his literary career, which was to remain a characteristic of Brecht.

In this context, it should be pointed out that Brecht's works were basically without an agenda from the start; it was a question of literature and its effects, not of conveying moral or political messages. From his early diary and in *Die Ernte*, there is no clear thematic direction, anything can stand next to anything else; nationalistic compositions alongside those with social themes, nature poetry alongside historicist literature.

Contradictions and oppositions in this respect do not play a role, because there aren't any actually – only the aesthetic dimension and the literary effect matter, not any "preoccupation" that is to be brought home to the reader through the poem.

to take the credit for texts that they hadn't written, and Brecht, as publisher of the paper, appeared to have a staff of authors. For the Augsburg schoolboy, the idealistic dimension of his own composition was a minor consideration. Completely materialistic, he seems to have only been interested in the utility value of his texts, which were instrumental in his goal of becoming a recognised author.

At an extremely early stage, then, he took a quite strategic, coolly calculating approach

And so it remained. From August 1914, following the beginning of the First World War, the schoolboy had the opportunity to publish in a "proper" medium for the first time, namely in two Augsburg daily papers. By early 1916, he had written almost forty articles. They appear to be in tune with the nationalistic Zeitgeist, with its glorification of war, while at the same time – for example in the *Augsburger Kriegsbriefen* (war letters) – containing a great deal of local colour. In fact, Brecht was at first not particularly interested in the war; but over time became increasingly sceptical towards it – principally because of the immense human suffering that it caused. The young Brecht only wrote his texts for the newspapers in this vein in order to be published, and that meant conforming to the prevailing war fever, otherwise the articles would have certainly been rejected. He was thus willing to make compromises. However, most of these articles demonstrably contain elements showing that he treats the nationalism ironically; operates on several literary levels and thereby distances himself from the political content of his texts.

The last of these texts, the Poem at the *Soldier's Grave*, appeared on 20th February 1916, and quite clearly shows resignation in the face of the terrors of war. No more were to follow until, with the *Song of the Railway*

ing literary virtuosity and diversity, their provocative character, their artificial distinctiveness, these poems show how intimately their author was entwined with his home city. We should never make the mistake of reading these texts as one-dimensional biography; nevertheless Augsburg is everywhere present in them, whether in the form of allusions to places, town squares, events and the adoration of women, or Brecht's friends, who are mentioned time and again in these poems. They breathe the spirit of the Augsburger "Plärrer" (the big fair that still takes place twice a year), the pubs of the old town, the wild, romantic Lech landscape, which Brecht had experienced with his circle of friends – the first "collective" – amongst whom he gained artistic inspiration but also encouraged and lastingly influenced others.

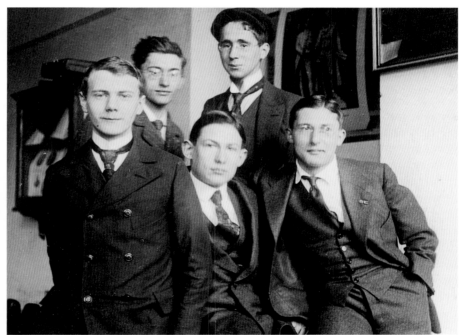

Gang from Fort Donald, printed on 13th July, 1916, Brecht achieved a completely new literary quality, making a quantum leap compared with his previous works.

While his works until then had been more or less literary finger exercises, he was now able to compose poetry that reached the level of the later Hauspostille, still his best known poetry anthology.

He wrote most of the poems for this collection in Augsburg. Besides their outstand-

One of the best known and most important poems of the *Hauspostille* is undoubtedly *The Legend of the Dead Soldier*. With inimitable virtuosity, Brecht uses it to criticise the foreign policy of the Wilhelmian Republic, for which no human sacrifice had been too great in its desperate bid for victory in the First World War. It is this text that was chiefly responsible for the National-Socialist government's decision to strip Brecht of his citizenship in 1934, for, among other things, ridiculing German front-line soldiers. It remained unnoticed for a long time that this poem, too, contains a specific Augsburg association as a determining element. Brecht tells of the fate of his friend Caspar Neher, who later – apart from his close collaboration with Brecht – was a highly regarded stage designer and was wounded in the war, and whom Brecht, with his Legend poem, wanted to warn again further service on the front line. Thus, besides social criticism, Brecht's own concerns and interests figure here – his gifted friend, whom he worries about and doesn't want to lose.

Of course, Brecht's dramatic production – after all, many know him first and foremost as a dramatist – had its beginnings in Augsburg. His first completed drama, the one-act play of just a few pages, *"The Bible"* was created in December 1913/January 1914, and was published in the student newspaper *Die Ernte*. It was to take another good five years until Brecht began to write literary history with *"Baal"* and *"Drums in the Night"*, which laid the basis for his winning the Kleist prize, for example, in 1924.

Naturally, these two pieces are not his best known, but they do impressively reflect his method of working, and, once again, the importance of Augsburg in Brecht's work. Both dramas draw on a large number of sources – the figure of the poet Baal living as a social outsider, for example, is by no means only oriented to Old Testament themes, but in his youth, Brecht really did know a vagabond called Johann Baal, who occasionally lived in Augsburg-Pfersee, and had been ruined by alcohol, but wrote poetry. And not least, the drama Baal is at one level also about its author, Brecht himself, who in all immodesty stylises himself here, too, as a brilliant anti-establishment author. The same is true of *"Drums in the Night"*. The principal figure of Andreas Kragler owes his name to the Josef Kragler, who returned injured from the war, and didn't live far from the Plärrer. And both pieces by the young Brecht demonstrate his independence of political standardisation, constraints or morals, but prove him, once again, to be a materialist in the narrowest sense. *"Drums in the Night"* is virtually a celebration of the attitude of caring about his own best interests while disregarding social ideals, and Brecht was all too ready to rework his *Baal,* to tame it down, when it

emerged that the original draft was too provocative to find a publisher and stage in his day – a flexibility in the interests of promoting his literary work that he was to retain, not least during his time in the GDR.

Two love affairs that moulded Brecht's life started in Augsburg. That with his childhood sweetheart and the mother of his first son Frank, the doctor's daughter Paula Banholzer, and that with the attractive but mediocre opera singer Marianne Zoff, who was to be his first wife. This union produced Brecht's daughter Hanne. She was born in 1923, when the poet was already in a relationship with Helene Weigel, later his second wife and artistic director of the Berlin Ensemble. However, Augsburg soon proved too small, too straightforward for the young Brecht to realise his great ambitions. He had to have the

access to writers' and artistic circles of larger cities, to put himself into the public eye, make contacts to publishers and theatre people if he was to raise his profile as a poet and live as such. Munich, too, where, from October 1917, he briefly studied medicine and German philology, visited the famous seminars of the drama theorist Artur Kutscher, and made acquaintances such as Lion Feuchtwanger, Karl Valentin and Otto Falckenberg, only appears as a stopover on his way to Berlin. He still retained contact with Augsburg during this time, not least through his close ties to Paula Banholzer and those allowed to count themselves among Brecht's Augsburg circle of friends. But even they increasingly lost importance for him. Other things became more important, urged him on his way to becoming a recognised writer. Though, during his Munich phase, he still often stayed in Augsburg, mainly commuting between the two cities, he was already preparing the ground in Berlin with frequent visits there, and we can consider September 1924 as the juncture. Brecht at last moved to Helene Weigel in Berlin; in summer, however, he was still in Augsburg for some weeks where his father – Brecht's mother had already died prematurely – kept a room free for him.

In the Berlin metropolis, Brecht went his way single-mindedly, quickly becoming part of the most exposed artistic and intellectual

Socialists forced him and his family into exile, which took him via several Scandinavian countries to the USA. It was now that he wrote his most important dramas: *The Good Person of Szechuan, Mother Courage and Her Children, Mr. Puntila and His Man Matti, Galileo, The Caucasian Chalk Circle.*

However, isolated from his homeland and the necessary contacts, he lacked the means to stage them appropriately. Most of Brecht's poetry was also written in exile. Many of the poems must be seen against the background of Brecht's opposition to Nazi barbarism, but others stand out for their timelessness. The most important poetry anthology at this time is the *Svendborger Gedichte.*

He also had difficulties in maintaining links to Augsburg; while in Scandinavian ex-

circles in the Weimar Republic. Some sensational works arose, such as the opera *Rise and Fall of the City of Mahagonny*. In 1932, after his world success with the *Threepenny Opera*, Brecht, who now considered himself a provocative but nevertheless typical writer, acquired a house in Utting on Ammersee, in what was even then an important recreation area for Augsburg.

However, he didn't have long to enjoy his new possession. At the end of February 1933, the accession to power by the National

ile, Brecht received visits from his old friend Rudolf Hartmann, his father and brother. We don't know what information channels the writer had with his homeland. We therefore don't know when Brecht first heard about his father's sudden death, which was the result of a traffic accident that had occurred weeks earlier.

We should take it for granted, rather than be surprised by the fact that Augsburg is ever present even in Brecht's later works. Direct mentions, numerous references to his former

sphere that are often not identified, can be found, but also longer literary reminiscences, such as *the Augsburg Chalk Circle,* the first of his *"Calendar Stories"*, and to some extent a prefiguration of the great drama *The Caucasian Chalk Circle.* The story doesn't only take place in Augsburg and its Swabian surroundings, but its central scene is held nowhere but in the Golden Room of the Augsburg Town Hall.

Brecht returned to Europe in 1947 and from 1949, together with his wife Helene Weigel, built up the Berlin Ensemble, with which, among other things, he staged model productions of his great pieces. This theatre became world famous within a short time; this is demonstrated not least by various guest performances abroad with spectacular successes. While none of his great dramas were created at this time, his poetic production continued unabated; The *Buckower Elegies,* with great poetical beauty, show us the melancholy of a prematurely aged Brecht, who seemed to be resigned, not least because of the restrictive political situation in the GDR.

On August 14, 1956, Brecht died of a heart attack and was interred in the graveyard in Dorotheenstadt, Berlin, within sight of his last apartment in Chausseestraße. He remained a controversial figure in both East and West Germany. His independence came from his adaptability, which emerged at an early stage, or perhaps better said, from his moral indifference, his materialism, which allowed him always to see in his poetry the artificial construct, the art work, not a vehicle for political maxims. But it also made him appear suspect and unsettling to all those who tried to fit him into clichés and templates, to make him into a model Marxist poet, or, depending on your point of view, into a disparaged representative of the GDR. However, the unique aesthetic qualities of his work put him beyond trends and ideologies, and made him into that what he wanted to be from his youth – a classic of German literature well beyond the frontiers of his homeland.

In Augsburg, as throughout Germany, there were problems with the acceptance of Brecht during the Cold War. The city's theatre regu-larly showed his works; the Augsburg press was always an open forum for discussing the playwright. Other initiatives, such as mounting a first commemorative plaque on the house where Brecht's was born were made on private initiative. During the sixties, "official" Augsburg cautiously began to accept its great son. In 1963, the city council made the decision to build up a Brecht collection in the Augsburg State and City Library – now the second biggest in the world – and made the financial resources available. In 1966, a street was named after the great son. In 1981, the house of Brecht's birth, which was still privately owned, was acquired by the City of Augsburg, renovated, and a memorial was established in the first floor, which was opened in 1985.

In the nineties, there were rapid developments at long last. In 1991, the Brecht research unit at the State and City Library was called into being and staffed. With its many publications about Brecht, and editions of his works, it is still one of the most important centres for theoretical examination of Brecht and his works, alongside the Bertolt Brecht archive in Berlin and the Bertolt Brecht group at the University of Karlsruhe. Since 1995, the Bert-Brecht-Award of the City of Augsburg has been awarded every three years.

On the 100th anniversary of his birth, the permanent exhibition in the Brecht house was redesigned from scratch and substantially extended. Augsburg has continually – most recently in 2006 for the 50th anniversary of Brecht's death – been able to present itself as the venue for the most widely exposed, internationally important congresses, festivals and other events.

That notwithstanding, an important role is still played by associations and private initiatives. The bookshop on the fruit market, with its "Brecht shop" is just one example of many. It is also the headquarters of the "Dreigroschenheft" ("Threepenny Paper"), an information medium with an international readership.

Thus, Brecht has long arrived back in Augsburg as regards the recognition of his internationally significant work.

TRACES OF THE BIG CITY

Augsburg, in the middle of the night from 10–11 May 1911: The sound of corks bursting out of bottles of champagne. Rockets and Bengal lights illuminating the night sky. Augsburg is having a party. A dream has come true, the dream of being a big city at long last. And the big day comes in 1911, the integration of local villages within the city of Augsburg boosting the population beyond that magic mark of 100,000 inhabitants. The citizens of a town have become the citizens of a city. More than 100 years have passed since the city was made part of Bavaria in its new form, developing from an old and rather tired Reichsstadt into a modern centre of industry. Now no longer the patricians, the owners of large factories determined the course of local politics, but rather the self-conscious industrial worker and the military in their parade uniforms to be seen and admired in the streets. They all demanded a new city, a city generous and modern in its style. Self-confident as usual, the citizens of Augsburg looked at the most outstanding metropolitan cities of Europe as their role models. The mediaeval wall round the city seen ultimately only as a kind of confining corset was torn down, new openings and passages being built in the new areas thus created, with large modern buildings along their sides. One of these main passages led to the station, another went straight to the city theatre. Cafés, coffee houses and magnificent apartment buildings soon

Left:
The old Stadtbad has kept its cheerful art deco atmosphere to this very day.

Top:
The Sauna and the sweat bath are furnished with richly ornamented tiles and fountains.

appeared on the scene. The new citizens created a new image of their city and developed a new image of themselves still to be admired today in two old photo studios in Augsburg. The well-to-do citizen at the photographer, wearing a shirt with a stiff collar, his wife and children around him, presenting himself in all his glory on the glass plate, his wife and children wearing their best dress and suits. It was Siemssen (Bahnhofstr. 10), the Royal Court Photographer, and Spalke und Kluge (K.-Adenauer-Allee 17 A), the Centre of Photographic Art, that catered for citizens in satisfying their new wish for prestige and style, both studios competing with one another through the use of the most advanced architecture, Oriental design full of fantasy here and French Art Deco ornaments there. Today both studios are empty and defunct – no good sign for the way Augsburg's citizens see themselves today. Between the two studios, right in the middle of the new axes leading through Augsburg, we find the central traffic junction, Königsplatz. All trams cross this large square and it is indeed the trams running through the city that provide the most dynamic impression of old and new Augsburg to this very day. One example is the tramline down Perlachberg to the old part of town. A colourful mixture of freshly refurbished gabled houses, pubs and Turkish greengrocer's shops now give the old city its special look. But this was not always the case. When the new upper class were trying out their new lifestyle in the large city further "uptown" around the turn of the century, the old part of town was the "opposite world", a greyish place full of houses and characterised by conditions not fit for human life. It was only an all-out effort in city

building and urbanisation that was able to thoroughly refurbish this part of town in recent decades.

But even the citizens around the turn of the century had responded to the sad conditions at the time. Benefiting from a generous donation by the Forster family in Augsburg, a modern washing and cleaning bath, the old Stadtbad (Leonhardsberg 15), was built right after the year 1900. A typical Jugendstil building, it was far more at the time then just a new structure with some unusual ornaments on the walls. Indeed, Jugendstil was acknowledged as the sign of a new feeling in life, of hygiene turning into reality, a new feeling of physical awareness. "Taking a bath" in those days was not just some kind of pastime, but rather a process of cleansing your body, of gaining and preserving your fitness. The large, brightly lit swimming halls were separated into a bath for women and a bath for men. Today this may be regarded as a bourgeois or even blatant symbol of segregation – but at the time it was a sign of relief, of liberalisation. At long last both men and women were able to take off their clothes, seeing themselves in the nude for the first time in the Roman-Irish steam bath and in the sauna. And there was even a dog's bath for man's best friend, allowing the dog and its owner to present themselves together in style on the stage of the big city. Today the old Stadtbad is open and accessible once again, regrettably in a very "purified", nondescript style, but the steam and sweat baths still exude the old spirit of a new age. It was also this ideal of the new, healthy human being that constantly urged on one of the most fascinating

Left: Cast-iron railings and spectacular glass windows in the auditorium of Kurhaus theatre.

Right: The design of the theatre is characterized by the great imagination of its architect Jean Keller and the extravagant taste of his client Friedrich Hessing, a truly self-made man of his time.

individuals in Augsburg around the turn of the century, Fritz Hessing. Hessing had come to Augsburg as a poor organ-builder, thus residing initially in the old part of town with many other craftsmen. And what he saw and experienced there must have been devastating. The narrow streets, poor hygiene, the lack of light and malnutrition had given children in the old city all kinds of deficiency symptoms. Hessing never forgot the sight of children crippled by rickets. Wanting to help these people, he developed all kinds of adventurous walking machines helping cripples to get up again and move forward in life. And focusing on all aspects, Hessing took people out of their old life and moved them into new, healthy surroundings. Just outside town he built a sanatorium with all the amenities of a large spa, creating everything himself, with sparse resources but great imagination. Today as in the past the tram still goes out to the Hessing Clinic in Gögginen, where getting off at Klausenberg you will experience the highlight of the entire facility, the Kurhaustheater, a theatre and winter garden where bedridden patients could be pushed out in wheelchairs from their wards right to the first row. Today this wonderful building is to be admired in all its glory, lavishly restored to perfection. At the time it was built in only one year on a small private budget and with the help of only simple craftsmen. Jean Keller, the architect, combined improvisation and the art of illusion to fulfil the wishes of his principal. The Kurhaustheater was the very heart of the spa, the actual healing and treatment facilities – today a modern orthopaedic clinic – only a short walk or one tram stop away. Other features still to be admired to

this very day are the small resort park with the tram running right through the middle, the Colonnade or Wandelhalle, Hessing's castle-like home and the magnificent spa chapel. Finished in French baroque style outside, the chapel is reminiscent inside of a neogothic stalactite cavern carved out of oak. Here again there is a gallery in the first row open to patients in a wheelchair and sufficient space lower down to roll in sickbeds. The idea, therefore, was to give patients – all patients, regardless of whether they were Catholic, Protestant or Russian Orthodox – the moral and spiritual stimulus they required. Indeed, Hessing even planned to build a special altar for affluent members of Russian nobility adjusting like a rotating stage to the needs of the respective religion. But like so many of his ideas, this concept fell victim to the stubbornness of his contemporaries.

Offering a kind of contrast to the posh Göggingen region in the south, the tram going west will take you to Pfersee, one of Augsburg's industrial suburbs on the other side of the Wertach River. And right after the bridge over the river you will find one of the most spectacular churches of its kind, the Catholic Church of the Heart of Jesus, near the tramlines. Starting work on this neoromanic building in 1908, architect Michael Kurz gave it all the splendour of German Jugendstil, the love for hearts of Jesus art running abound all over Europe at the time adding a flair of moving, naive sentimentality to this ornamental glory. One example is to be found among the figures painted in the choir area, an oversized Indian chief next to the usual heathen tribes, who

Using the full panoply of a magnificent Catholic staging the interior design finds its climax in the entirely ornamented choir with its gilt tabernacle altar.

might just as well have come out of one of the books written by Karl May. And this is no coincidence, since Karl May had been in Augsburg in the very same year 1908, also the year in which *Winnetous Erben* was first published as a serial in the then renowned Augsburger Postzeitung. These were the years full of hope prior to World War I in which the dream of the good and kind-hearted »savage« in the middle of this industrial suburb became reality. Alas, this ideal of the new, good human being only persisted for a few more years, the outbreak of war destroying all these dreams. We see this in particular when beholding the paintings in the Church of the Heart of Jesus: The artist who painted the choir area fell in Verdun, new artists continued his work along the long walls of the house. And here martial henchmen dominate the way of the Cross, a Gullible Fritz wearing his steel helmet also making his appearance in the scene. Right at the end an ordinary soldier in uniform painted on the pulpit marks the end of the church building and the end of a chapter in city life seeking to offer people a better existence in their new, healthy city open to the world.

Ⓐ Herz-Jesu-Church
Built in 1907/09 in Art Deco-Style, architect Michael Kurz, Augsburg.

Ⓑ Old Stadtbad – Art Deco Style, built in 1902/03 by Municipal Building Magistrate Fritz Steinhäußer.

Ⓒ Royal Court photographer Siemssen – Back Building in 10, Bahnhofstr., former Photographer's studio, ornamented in French Art nouveau style.

Ⓓ Spalke and Kluge's Centre of Photographic Art
Back Building in 17 A, Konrad-Adenauer-Allee, former Photographer's studio, Oriental-Moorish style.

Ⓔ Göggingen Kurhaus Theatre
6, Klausenberg. Built in 1885 by architect Jean Keller for his client Friedrich Hessing. Important monument of German Engineering. Rendered brick building with integrated iron construction and large-scale windows. Heavily damaged after a fire in 1972, it was reopened in 1996 as a theatre and congress hall.

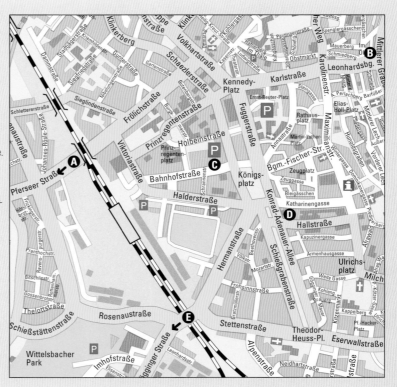

The "glass palace" (see previous page) may be Augsburg's most important public 20th century building. The architectural masterpiece built to the plans of Philipp Jakob Manz (1861–1936) is the first major steel-skeleton construction in Germany. As a jewel of the textile quarter, which was so important to the city at the time, it originally accommodated Factory IV (bank mill) of the Mechanische Baumwollspinnerei und Weberei Augsburg (a cotton

ifest its monumental effect in full, particularly when approached from the south. The unbroken rhythm of the massive window façades at the north and south extends from the ground floor to the roof, and gives the architecture a unique, fascinating and unmistakable character, which is visible from afar.

The building was owned by the city for many years, before it was sold to the for-

The Exhibition "A walk in New York" shows work by American artists of the 20th century. Shown here, pictures by Robert Motherwell (right) and Andy Warhol (rear).

spinning and weaving company). When the massive pioneering work had been completed, the factory came on stream in 1910 and was used for this purpose well into the last quarter of the 20th century.

The glass palace now stands architecturally rather disconnected, directly on the circular road, one of the functionally very practical, but architecturally uneasy feeder roads to and from the present A8 autobahn. Nevertheless, the building can man-

mer building contractor Ignaz Walter. His private art collection and an own gallery were moved into the 2nd and 3rd floor of the building, while the storeys below were leased to various companies and service providers.

Following protracted and complicated negotiations between the city of Augsburg and the present building owner, a contract was concluded to permit the creation, at long last, of a state art gallery and a new city art gallery on the still-empty ground floor. In May 2006, the Staatsgalerie Moderne Kunst (state gallery of modern art, a branch of the Pinakothek der Moderne in Munich) and the H2 – Zentrum für Gegenwartskunst (centre for contemporary art) were ready to open to the public on the capacious ground floor of the glass palace.

The Staatsgalerie, though pursuing a fundamentally new concept, is a successor to contemporary art. Many ventures of this kind have been realised internationally – particularly in recent decades. Outstanding projects, such as the Hallen für Neue Kunst, Schaffhausen, the Zentrum für Kunst und Medientechnologie in Karlsruhe or the spectacular former turbine hall in London, which now houses the Tate Modern, are just a few examples. Compared with these and many other building complexes with a similar function, how-

the former Kunsthalle at Wittelsbacher Park, while the H2 – Zentrum für Gegenwartskunst, represents Augsburg's first-ever own municipal museum, reflecting regional, national and international contemporary art, and presents it to the public for critical examination in temporary exhibitions.

There is nothing new about reusing historical industrial architecture as museums and galleries, particularly for presenting ever, the Augsburg glass palace has some unique and entirely unprecedented features of its own, namely the many closely spaced columns and almost uninterrupted window façades on the south and north sides, offering very little "natural" scope to hang exhibits.

Against this background of a completely preserved structure that is now a listed building, and its distinctive light-flooded architecture, therefore, the planning of the H2 followed a simple but clear maxim from the start. Namely, not to crowd the space with fixed partitions, despite the restricted facilities for hanging, but to respect its unique character, and respond to it in the context of contemporary art.

H2 – the "H" stands for hall – is both a gallery and a platform for temporary exhibitions. Firstly, the young art collection of

The Italian media artist Fabrizio responded to the rooms of the H2 with his space-filling installation LAVA, in the form of a first artistic intervention and as the first individual exhibition project. Here, Plessi realised a single monumental floor work.

An interior landscape accessible to visitors, comprising 30 piles of basalt stone slabs, stacked on one another and fitted with video monitors, taking up the enti-

the Augsburger Kunstsammlungen is presented in temporary exhibitions. Secondly, internationally famous artists "work" with the space through temporary individual exhibition projects, making references to it in their works, and making the visitors' sense of space into an eternally new, stimulating experience. Sensing the unique generosity of this fascinating hall, its "breathing", and moving in the extensive art space are already a pleasure for many visitors.

re space of the great exhibition hall. Because visitors can wander around in this spatial work of art, the space itself was also renewed and perceived in a different way, entirely as intended by the artist and in keeping with the curatorial concept, which places the visitor's spatial experience at centre stage.

But back to the collection. The H2 presents a collection that is still young and still in progress. Since the collection and temporary exhibition areas have deliberately not been separated from one another as a result of the current room situation, the presentation of the collection is no more static than the self image of the house itself. That means that new productions at greater regular intervals will result in a change of scene, create new dialogues between the art works and present them in ever new constellations. Thus, visitors can be introduced to the art of their day in exciting, one which takes into account the transdisciplinary networking of the arts, in which the classical demarcation of familiar art genres are now dissolved for artists themselves.

Thus, besides exciting examples of modern painting, there are also photography, electronic art, space and sound installations that are not separated from one another according to groups, but presented

H2 – Zentrum für Gegenwartskunst. Rupprecht Geiger. Title: Pinc contra Orange.

citing, varied and continually surprising new ways.

The time frame here – with the exception of the painting "circular form with luminous colour" by Rupprecht Geiger, which was created in 1957 – stretches from the 1980s until the present day. The characterising feature is not, as in many other houses, a collection focus, a specialisation on painting, graphic arts, sculpture or other individual disciplines, but, on the con-

contextually and in a direct, sensual exchange with one another.

Many of the exhibited artistic work originated in projects that artists have realised in Augsburg dealing directly with the current, historical and topographical situation. Thus, the Munich artist duo Empfangshalle (Corbinian Böhm and Michael Gruber) asked four attendants of the Neue

pp. 176/177: The factory castle, built 1895–98.

THOMAS ELSEN | 175

Galerie im Höhmannhaus – where their project took place in Augsburg – to form a temporary fountain on Maximilianstraße in which each living "fountain statue" would carry one of its own personal attributes in its hand. The resulting photo series Aufseherbrunnen (attendant fountain) is a contemporary comment, not without a twinkle in its eye, of the great tradition of the historical show fountain in Maximilianstraße, stimulating us to reflect on our

brary" in the Augsburg Hofgarten, which was also installed simultaneously in the Neue Galerie im Höhmannhaus. This, too, has been recorded by artistic photography, which the H2 presents in its collection. Thus, besides aesthetic reflection, visitors are also presented with a part of the most recent Augsburg art history.

The H2 is thus a gallery, temporary exhibition hall and experimental house

The glass palace also houses the Kunstmuseum Walter and the famous Galerie Noah (exhibition with Georg Baselitz, 2007).

basic attitude to (historical and contemporary) art. The Basel artist Leta Peer hung her painting Swiss Mountain Landscape in the building site during the renovation of the Schaezler Palace, and then photographed it, and so created a fascinating composition of painting, photography, free artistic work and also a document of the actual situation there. The New York artists Clegg & Guttmann, on the invitation of the Association of Contemporary Art (GfG), created an "Open Public Li-

in one. Regular guided tours for adults and, especially for children, concerts, films, performances and museum educational activities make the gallery a truly living experience that appeals to all generations.

Along with the top-quality selection of international modern art from the holdings of the Pinakothek der Moderne in Munich, that makes the H2 a nucleus for living contemporary culture in Augsburg.

The publicly accessible library of the H2 also represents an additional information and education portal for everyone. It is a library dedicated to the art of the 20th and 21st centuries.

In the context of a prepared cooperation with the Augsburg University library, an information platform has already been created here that is already widely used by students and scholars, but also interested laypersons, and provides active support to the H2 as an informative and living element of its exhibition activities.

Next door, the Artothek, run by the private Association of Contemporary Art (GfG) has also moved into its new home. It is a non-profit-making association, which is committed to promoting contemporary art. The Artothek allows citizens living in Augsburg and its environs to borrow original contemporary graphic works. This service, too, is extremely popular and complements the H2's programme.

Simultaneously with the H2, the branch gallery of the Munich Pinakothek der Moderne has opened in the hall opposite. With the title "a walk through New York", works by famous artists such as Robert Morris, Robert Motherwell, Robert Rauschenberg, John Cage, Andy Warhol, Dan Flavin and Donald Judd are assembled here. These artists determined the direction of art after the Second World War, which has gone down in history under the names Abstract Expressionism, Pop Art or Minimal Art. The loft-like character of the high, light-filled rooms of the glass palace proves an ideal setting for presentation of the large-format American art works since 1950. The subsidiary of the Pinakothek der Moderne has also conceived itself as a temporary exhibition.

In 1770, Johann Heinrich von Schüle founded his calico factory at the Rotes Tor modelled on a baroque castle. Now it is used by the technical university for design.

After years of hard wrangling, another newly established museum in the former Augsburg textile district now stands immediately in front of this house. The Bayerische Textil- und Industriemuseum (tim), which is currently in construction, is, according to its own information, due to be opened in 2009. It will occupy extensive halls in a building complex of the Augsburger Kammgarnspinnerei (AKS) from 1836, which congenially performs

In their importance, the new museums in the former Augsburg textile district not only enrich the Augsburg museumscape, but also open up entirely new horizons. The textile district, an area of great historical, urban architectural and creative potential, is slowly awakening from its long hibernation.

The art galleries in the glass palace and tim museum may be setting in motion the

This jacquard loom in the tim museum weaving shop is producing a retro flower pattern from the 1970s again (bottom).

the function of a museum. tim is championing the cause of appraising the textile history of Augsburg, Swabia and Bavaria, which has so far been neglected by commentators, and at the same time of conceiving a contemporary theme park taking into account the view of modern visitors. This will include functioning industrial machines that can be used by visitors, as well as industry, design and art exhibitions and – already in preparation – fashion shows.

resurrection and vital re-formation of an entire city district, which offer undreamt-of potential – elegantly and through profound confrontation with the still largely unknown history and identity of the city.

The new galleries not only represent first class cultural centres for this purpose. They also offer the ideal conditions for experiencing city culture, history and atmosphere beyond the periphery of Maximilianstraße.

Book from the NAK pattern collection: It shows the Turkish red print and the variety of patterns produced in the heyday (1788–1877).

Neckerchief with floral and geometric patterns (right).

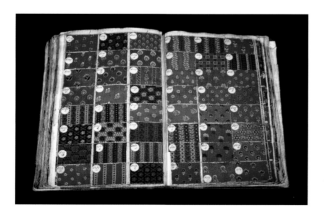

Ⓐ Glass Palace
Mechanic Cotton Weaving Mill, Building IV (Aumühle). Built in 1909/10 by Thormann and Stiefel according to plans by the archictect Manz. A historical heritage of European importance.

Ⓑ Factory Castle
Building III (Proviantbach) of Augsburg Spinning and Weaving Mill. Built in 1895–98 by Thormann and Stiefel according to plans by Carl Arnold Séquin-Bronner.

Ⓒ Proviantbach District
Typical late 19th-century housing estates for the workers of the Mechanic Cotton Weaving Mill, Building III (Proviantbach). Twenty three-storey brick houses, built from 1895 on, at a close distance to the plant premises.

Ⓓ Former Schüle Cotton Factory
later Textilwerke Nagler and Son. Shaped like a horse-shoe, it offers a façade worthy of a castle. Built in 1770/72 by Leonhard Christian Mayr. One of the most important buildings in European industrial history.

Ⓔ Augsburger Kammgarnspinnerei
Founded in 1836, from 1845 on new plants, in use up to this day, were built alongside Schäfflerbach River.

Ⓕ Power station of Stadtbach Cotton Mill
Built in 1902 at the north end of Wolfzahnau.

Ⓖ Municipal Fountains at Hochablass
Machines and engines by MAN. In use since 1879.

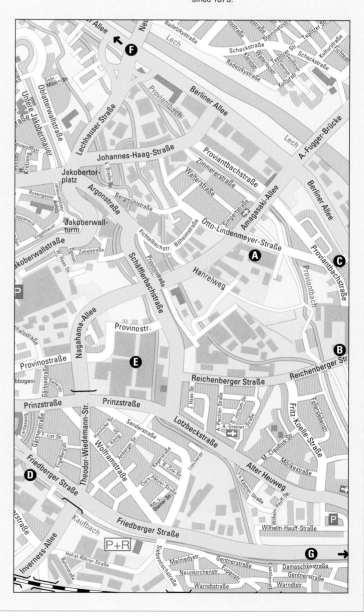

Flourishing City. There is an appeal to being spared the sky-scrapers and multi-lane high-way junctions.

HOW THE PRESENT NEVER WAS

AND HOW THE FUTURE
COULD BE

HOW THE PRESENT NEVER WAS AND HOW THE FUTURE COULD BE

A not entirely serious but not entirely unserious look at a beautiful city, whose potential is greater than its realities

We look back at Augsburg's glorious past with shining eyes. But our vision dulls markedly when we turn to the present and the future. The word "decline" suggests itself – once a world centre, now a province. But let us take a second, slightly different, look at history past, present and future. It could be worthwhile.

What might have been if Augsburg had continued in its dynamic role as one of the world centres of commerce, finance and culture to the present day?

Here are a few not entirely serious, but also not entirely unserious, answers to this fascinating question.

The metropolis of the Fuggers and Welsers would have developed into a modern megacity, a world centre of commerce, finance, and culture by modern standards. What would this Augsburg have looked liked?

We would see the glass highrisers of great international banks, let us say, on Halderstraße. "Halderstraße" would then be a household word, like Wall Street and the City of London. Industrial and commercial giants would have their headquarters, let us say, along Annastraße. The highest skyscrapers in the world would stand in Augsburg, raised to compete with Shanghai, Dubai, Kuala Lumpur and Chicago.

In the romantic old city, hidden between the high-rise blocks, cheek by jowl with Augsburg's lively Chinatown, high-class designer shops and international star chefs would compete for the sophisticated clientele.

Augsburg's theatres and museums would be world ranking and of world reputation. International artists and authors would commute between New York, London and Augsburg. Diana Damrau and Anna Netrebko would be habitués at the Augsburg Opera, an architectural and acoustic marvel.

The Augsburger Allgemeine would be the New York Times of Europe.

The Transrapid would link Greater Augsburg to Greater Paris. Munich, once an independent, charming medium-sized city on the Isar would long have been incorporated into the metropolitan area of the Augsburg megacity, with its more than ten million residents.

Wouldn't it be wonderful?

Yes and no. In the slums of the Augsburg megacity, there would be several murders every night. Drug barons would have made some districts into no-go areas for the police. Schwabing, now a dangerous district, would be known as the Bronx of Greater Augsburg. The latest international hit musical the "Bavarian Westside Story" would be running there.

Most of the good citizens of Greater Augsburg would have moved out to the quieter countryside, preferably along the lakes. They would take for granted the three-hour commute between the office and their suburbs to avoid the stresses and dangers of the megacity.

The next summit meeting of eminent United Nations experts on the theme of "crisis and management of the mega-cities", most recently in Shanghai, would now be taking place in Greater Augsburg. Since this would be the ideal place for case studies on the downside of supermetropolises and their European variant.

In short, modern global metropolises offer everything, joy and horror scenarios. Fantastic as it might have been in some respects, it would also have been almost unbearable if our city had retained its role as a world metropolis after the Thirty Years War and continued to develop at the same pace.

World metropolises and quality of life are two different things. It's only in exceptional cases that the two come together.

What often used to be sneered at as "the provinces" must now often be called a blessing in disguise.

But you don't have to be the most backward of provinces. No, the second rank in importance, seems to me to be an excellent place to be. Life is good here. World affairs with all their rewards are within easy reach. And you don't have to put up with the continual punishments that the great metropolises administer nowadays. You have the best of both worlds.

But what would the future be like of an Augsburg that was self-consciously aware of and enjoyed the advantages of the second

Modern city. Clear forms. clear colours. great calm. Modernity doesn't always mean noise and chaos.

rank, and proudly represented this status to the outside world?

Here are a few not entirely unserious, but also not entirely serious, answers to this fascinating question.

Self-confidence means not covering up the charms of the somewhat more prominent neighbour, but taking advantage of them. They make Augsburg even more attractive. Whether you call it Greater Munich, the Metropolitan Region of Munich or the heart of Bavaria is entirely secondary – Munich is fantastic, if you live in Augsburg.

The world metropolis of Augsburg is past history, and as history is perhaps the proudest of modern Augsburg's strong points. But Augsburg doesn't get its strong points just from history. They are to be found everywhere in the present. Industry, science, culture, sport, leisure, architecture, location, tourism, interesting people? We've got it all. This is the wealth from which Augsburg can create its future.

Here are a just a few typical glimpses into the future.

Let us start with the most tangible – Augsburg the sports city. After ice hockey and water sports, Augsburg – despite some setbacks – becomes a solid force in football once again: FC Augsburg, Bundesliga, a new stadium.

Sport, football at least, has given the city and region a fresh impetus. The atmosphere, attitude to life, optimism, the nationwide reputation as a city of sport, the economic effects of a sporting success story? All that is a thrilling future.

Industry and transport: After the great age of Augsburg, our city enjoyed a second flowering in the 19th and 20th centuries as an industrial site, from the textile industry to mechanical engineering. Some of that disappeared again, some was dismantled, but enough has remained, and new industries started, to create the future.

From the variety of the economic future potential, we can focus on three strong points – environmental expertise, mechatronics and fibre composites.

What will the environmental city of Augsburg look like in the future?

It will not be a city just of environmental authorities, environmental organisations and fine plans.

Youthful City. Where recent history forms the backdrop, a relaxed new generation practices for the future.

In the Augsburg of the future, commitment to the future will shine from every roof. The city administration goes all out for the environment. Solar energy is quite literally on the roofs of all public and many private buildings. Why should Augsburg in Germany not be famous as the city of solar energy?

In transport policy, the bicycle, this most environmentally friendly means of propulsion, is completely rediscovered. An attractive, well-planned, diverse and safe system of cycle paths convinces many to leave their car at home and pedal briskly through the city.

Car drivers no longer have a reason to curse cyclists as reckless road hogs. And cyclists no longer need to see themselves as mounted front-line fighters against a superior enemy force of car drivers. In short, Augsburg becomes the Münster of the south.

With mechatronics and modern materials technology, something finally becomes reality that was talked about for years, but far too little done – close, trusting and profitable cooperation between industry and the universities. Company executives and CEOs on one side and university professors on the other increasingly learn to speak one another's languages.

They discover that profits and science are not opposites but complementary partners. The cultural bureaucrats give universities a free hand without intervening. That is good for everyone concerned.

Thanks to the better cooperation between researchers, politicians and industrialists, a market-oriented mechatronics and materials competency grows up in and around Augsburg that is unparalleled in Germany. The Lech Valley gains an excellent reputation in Europe as a region of pioneering materials technology and materials development and marketing.

The environment, mechatronics and new materials are such attractive fields of expertise that they not only keep modern, forward-looking, well-trained people in the region, but bring them here in hordes.

Leisure and culture: Active people earning good money in modern jobs here are spoilt by the Lech Valley not only with excellent workplaces but also with an excellent variety of leisure and culture facilities, and a southern lifestyle.

Power City. High-tech thrives best where you can enjoy life after a successful day's work.

The historic inner city is entirely dedicated to the pleasures of life. Restrictive regulations are reduced to a minimum. What the natives had maintained all along is now spreading throughout Germany – Augsburg really is the northernmost Italian city, with a flair that could be just as much at home south of the Alps.

The eternal beauty of the nearby Alps and the lifestyle of the people continue to ensure that the city will retain its friendly Bavarian-Swabian character despite the italianitá.

Art and culture thrive as a collaboration between Augsburg and Munich. The smaller city is skilfully developing its own cultural accent and cleverly exploiting the attractions of the bigger city. It is thus creating a varied offering for all needs. And after every trip to Munich, they're glad to return to Augsburg, because it is nice here, and because housing costs stay so reasonable here that you can still afford such cultural experiences.

Augsburg itself is proliferating more than ever with its great cultural themes – from Mozart and Brecht to "Peace", which, historically speaking, has never been at home anywhere so much as with us.

From this triad, an overall scheme develops and is combined with an audacious contemporary art that inspires all citizens. All this is bundled in a professional market strategy. Augsburg becomes a cultural magnet.

Modern artists of international standing are drawn to Augsburg. They scramble to set up their sculptures here. In this way, they consolidate the city's reputation as a place with an exemplarily open-minded and liberal attitude towards avant-garde art. This reputation and the available abundance attract ever more visitors.

In the Augsburger Allgemeine newspaper, we read more and more reports of residents complaining about the swelling stream of tourists.

The newly elected mayoress of the future retorts: "Those are exactly the worries that we need." Located at the centre of the Romantic Road, between Rothenburg and the royal castles, Augsburg is the destination for many hundreds of thousands of Chinese tourists. Prices in Augsburg shops are displayed in euros and yuan.

Trade: The general dynamism also gives a new independent dynamism to trade in the

City of the South. Where you can see the Alps, the Bavarian way of life is mixed with a hint of Italy.

city. Creative shopkeepers enthral the public. Where they once spoke of a vicious cycle of decline, they now speak of a virtuous cycle of dynamism.

Munich residents who find exactly what they are looking for in the compact, excellent selection of first-class Augsburg shops can be heard to say quietly, "the best thing about Munich is the train to Augsburg."

And that is a view of a not completely impossible future of our city. How can this future become reality?

Perhaps by Augsburg's political powers joining forces in the city's interest in a way unprecedented throughout Germany. They fight for Augsburg professionally and creatively with nationwide impact.

The city and state stand shoulder to shoulder in the knowledge that they are only strong together. Personal vanities and the party lines are only incidental. What matters is the future of Augsburg.

Excellent ties develop between the Augsburg city authorities and national government. In Augsburg, many bold future plans are hatched and developed for realisation. They are so good that, in Munich, they have no choice – they agree enthusiastically.

Private initiative is joyfully supported by the local authorities, and is even demanded. Anyone wanting to become established as an entrepreneur immediately receives an offer of property, and all the necessary approvals, which have been reduced to a minimum, in double-quick time.

If all this could come together so wonderfully, then Augsburg has a glowing future ahead.

If only!

Could it really come true? Or do we have to soberly commit the vision to the realms of fantasy? On the principle of "and they all lived happily ever after."

Fairy tale or possibility?

Perhaps the future lies somewhere between the two. It will probably never be quite as good as described here. But perhaps this painted vision is somewhat more than a fairy tale.

One thing is certain, there are good prospects not only among the big players, but also in the comfortable second rank. That is Augsburg's real hope for the future.

Photos

REINHARD EISELE

Diploma in design and photography, born in Augsburg and photographer for high-class illustrated books (India, Hawaii, the Engadine, Tuscany, Bali, U.S.A, California, Dominican Republic, Caribbean and Upper Bavaria), and author of numerous books on photography (travel photography, architectural photography and landscape photography). Besides travel photography also experience as publicity and reportage photographer. His customers include industrial companies, publicity agencies, insurance companies, banks, automotive, sports and fashion companies and many publishing houses and editorial offices. Published in GEO, Merian, GEO-Saison, National Geographic, Fotomagazin, Photographie, Zeit-Magazin, Stern, Spiegel, Die Welt, Focus, Süddeutsche Zeitung and many others. Reinhard Eisele is also the founder and owner of the picture agencies Project Photos GmbH and Eisele-Photos.

Book Design

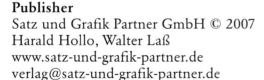

HARALD HOLLO

Born in Stuttgart in 1948, grew up in Augsburg, married, three children. Trained as compositor, master craftsman examination in 1972. Lived abroad in Zurich and Vienna. Studied graphic design at the Werkkunstschule Augsburg; specialist teacher in printing technology at the Grafische Akademie Munich. Managing director of Satz und Grafik Partner since 1986. Producer of several art books. Published works: "Augsburg – Cityscapes", "Schwaben – Blickpunkte", "Vergangene Burgen und Herrensitze", "Munich – Cityscapes", "Das Kriegsende in Bayerisch-Schwaben 1945", "Burgen, Schlösser und Residenzen in Bayerisch-Schwaben", "Die Stauden – Porträt einer Landschaft in Bayerisch-Schwaben".

Publisher
Satz und Grafik Partner GmbH © 2007
Harald Hollo, Walter Laß
www.satz-und-grafik-partner.de
verlag@satz-und-grafik-partner.de

Typesetting and lithography
Satz und Grafik Partner GmbH

English translation
chapters 1–17, 19, 20 and foreword
by Stephen Wood

Printer
Kessler Druck + Medien

The Authors

ANGELA BACHMAIR M.A.

Born in 1949 in Buchloe/Allgäu, Germany
School-leaving certificate in 1969, Augsburg
Studied social sciences in Erlangen and Munich;
Magister Artium 1975
Worked in adult education and journalism in Munich and Kassel
Editor with the Augsburger Allgemeine since 1986
Married, two grown-up children, two young grandchildren

DR. LOTHAR BAKKER

Born in 1949 in Bergisch-Neukirchen and, from childhood, "rooted in the soil" on his parents' farm. After taking his school leaving certificate, studied Protestant theology and history at the University of Bonn. Had formative encounters with the "Romans" in Cologne in 1967 and in Rome itself in 1968. In 1981 gained his doctorate in Bonn in provincial Roman archaeology, ancient history and geology. Worked in the Land Bureau for the Conservation of Historic Monuments in Koblenz; "city archaeologist" in Augsburg since 1982 and also head of the Roman museum since 1990. Centre of life: family (three daughters) and work, which really means vocation. Found the first "stone of life" in his home town (wife Anneliese), transplanted to the soil of Roman Augsburg as an archaeological excavator, and associated with a second "stone of life", the "Augsburg Victory Altar" of 260 AD.

GÖTZ U. BECK

was born in Munich in 1960. Spent his childhood and youth in the northern Swabian town of Donauwörth. After training in the hotel and hospitality trade, spent his military service in Ulm and Dillingen. Then visited the hotel college in Heidelberg, qualifying as state-examined hotel business administrator. Subsequently studied business administration at Munich technical university, specializing in tourism. Then he was tourism director of Bad Mergentheim, the biggest spa in Baden Württemberg. Here, he held responsibility for the areas of tourism, culture and business development. Since 1998, he has held the post of tourism director in Augsburg, where, as director of the Regio-Augsburg Tourismus GmbH, he is responsible for developing and supporting tourism in the city of Augsburg and rural districts of Augsburg and Aichach-Friedberg.

RAINER BONHORST

Born in 1942 in Nuremberg
Editor with the Westdeutsche Allgemeine Zeitung
Correspondent in London and Washington for the Westdeutsche Allgemeine Zeitung and the Augsburger Allgemeine
Deputy editor-in-chief of the Westdeutsche Allgemeine Zeitung
Editor in chief of the Augsburger Allgemeine since July 1, 1994

DR. THOMAS ELSEN

Born in Bitburg in 1958, grew up in Leverkusen. Studied art history, philosophy and pract. theology in Cologne and Bonn, DAAD scholarship at the Institute of Art History in Florence. Publicity work for the Cologne Art Association and Sony Deutschland as part of the retrospective "video sculpture", Cologne (Art association) – Berlin (Congress Hall) – Zurich (Art House) 1988–89. Art history director of the first exhibition of the Free State of Saxony after German reunification "Georgius Agricola", Chemnitz (Art Collections) – Bochum (German Mining Museum) – Prague (National Technical museum) 1993–94. Since 2002 deputy director of Kunstsammlungen und Museen Augsburg, since 2006 head of the H2 - Centre for Contemporary Art in the Glass Palace.

DR. CHRISTOPH EMMENDÖRFFER

born in 1965 in Meppen. Studied European Art History, Classical Philology, Classical Archaeology and Modern History in Heidelberg and Bologna. Since 1998, director of the Maximilian Museum and responsible for the reconception of Maximilian Museum, which was reopened in November 2006. Curator of the exhibitions "Adriaen de Vries. Augsburg's Glory – Europe's Fame" (2000) and "Silver of the Tsars, Augsburg Silver from the Kremlin" (2008), collaboration with the exhibition "When Peace was Possible. 450 Years of Augsburg Religious Peace".

PROF. DR. HANS FREI

Born in 1937 in Augsburg, grew up in Augsburg and Bobingen. Studied geography, history and German philology in Munich, state examination as a teacher at grammar schools, doctorate and research assistant at the Geographical Institute of the University of Munich. From 1970 to 1987, full-time local history curator for the region of Swabia, concentrating on: monument conservation, folklore, cultural landcape. Founded the district museums of Oberschönenfeld, Maihingen and Naichen. From 1988 to 2002, museum director for the region of Swabia. Publisher and author of numerous publications in the fields of monument conservation, museology, cultural studies with an emphasis on Swabia. Member of the board of the Swabian Research Association. Part-time lecturer and honorary professor of cultural geography and cultural studies at the Universities of Augsburg and Munich.

JUDITH GARDNER

Born in 1971. While studying journalism also attended the German School of Journalism in Munich; later worked in various media, such as children's television. By this circuitous route, joined the ensemble of the Augsburger Puppenkiste in 1999, where she found her dream job in the puppet theatre. Occasionally writes various kinds of texts for the Puppenkiste.

FRANZ HÄUSSLER

Born in 1940 in a centuries-old former vicarage of the Teutonic Order in Lauterbach, on the border of Zusamtal. It is impossible to say now whether his early interest in history was the result of his history-steeped birthplace, in the shadow of the church and brewery, or thanks to the historian Dr. Layer at the Dillingen Grammar School, who inspired a generation of scholars. An Augsburger since 1955 – and liked it more from year to year. Worked for over three decades for Swabia's leading newspaper. Publications since 1980: several thousand pictures and newspaper articles, five books. Several exhibitions. Themes: mainly Augsburg's history from "A" for archaeology to "Z" for Zerstörung (destruction). Principle: "Tell and show it like it was – without nostalgia or sentimentality".

ULRICH HEISS

lives and works as an occasional writer in Augsburg. His range comprises three volumes with histories of Ernie and Bert from Sesame Street, an architectural guide book on the architecture of the 19th and 20th century in Augsburg, publicity texts for a European hotel chain and articles for daily newspapers and Bavarian TV. As head of the architectural museum of Swabia and the kunsthaus kaufbeuren, he has been able to initiate and realise many exhibitions on contemporary architecture and art. His first theatre play, a rustic farce, is currently waiting for its debut performance.

DR. JÜRGEN HILLESHEIM

born in 1961 in Koblenz, studied Catholic theology, German philology and philosophy in Mainz, since 1991 head of the Brecht research centre at the State and City Library of Augsburg. Author of numerous books and articles about Thomas Mann, National Socialist literature and Bertolt Brecht, co-editor of the Brecht-Jahrbuch (almanac) and the book series "Der neue Brecht", publisher of Brecht's work until 1916.

ANDREA KÜMPFBECK

Born – and deeply rooted – in old-traditional Lower Bavaria. First journalistic experience with reports about the rabbit-breeding association and the school concert for the local newspaper. Immediately after her school-leaving certificate in Landau/Isar, trainee and editorial experience with the Landshuter Zeitung. Studied German and English philology in the most beautiful city in Bavaria, Regensburg. After detours into the cultural department and a short stop with the German-Jewish exile newspaper "Aufbau" in New York, arrived in Swabia. First with the Allgäuer Zeitung, since 2000 in the second most beautiful and greenest city in Bavaria as a reporter with the Augsburger Allgemeine. Since then, continually on the move – in Swabia, Bavaria and throughout the world: at the Tsunami in South East Asia, with the Pope in Rome, at the earthquake in Pakistan or the flood catastrophe in Nepal.

EVA LEIPPRAND

Born in Erlangen in 1947, grew up in Munich. Studied (English and History) in Würzburg and Munich, with an intermediate year in England. Moved to Stuttgart by marriage. Spent the 17 years there partly as a secondary school teacher, partly with the education of two children. In Augsburg since 1989 as a freelance author. Works in various civic initiatives, chairperson of the Forum Augsburg lebenswert (1994 to 2002). Town councillor from 1996 to 2002; since 2002, head of cultural affairs and third mayoress of the city of Augsburg.

MANUELA MAYR

Manuela Mayr, born in 1954 in Waldshut am Hochrhein. Wonderful childhood in South Baden, heavily influenced by Lower-Bavarian grandparents. Active journalist since her school days. After her school-leaving certificate, spent years teaching and travelling in Berlin and Venice. Professionally "stranded" at the Augsburger Allgemeine, where she works as an editor on the "Bavaria and the World" desk. She has put down private roots in Kühbach, old Bavaria. With her husband, from East Allgäu by birth, she enjoys country life there in a former farmhouse that was even mentioned in documents before the Thirty Years War.

DR. CHRISTOF METZGER

is an art historian and was born on November 13, 1968, in Nördlingen and, as shown by numerous publications on late-mediaeval art history of this former imperial city, is still to this day a declared career Nördlinger. After studying art history and archaeology, was stranded more by accident in Augsburg, and worked for many years as an exhibition curator and scientist for art collections and museums in Augsburg and Munich. As a passionate dilettante organist and cembalist, considered a connoisseur of 18th century music, he curated the large "Mozart's World" jubilee exhibition in the Augsburg Schaezler Palace in 2006, which went into several extensions.

DR. CHRISTOF PAULUS

born in 1974 in Augsburg, studied German, history and Latin in Munich and Rome. In 2005, he gained his doctorate for a thesis on "The Count Palatine Office in Bavaria in the Early and High Middle Ages". He is a teacher at the Friedberg Grammar School.

PROF. DR. BERND ROECK

born in Augsburg, he was director of the German Study Centre in Venice from 1986 until 1990, and from 1991 until 1999 was professor of mediaeval and modern history at the University of Bonn, from 1996 until 1999 he was also general secretary of the Italian-German Centre Villa Vigoni (Loveno/Como). Since 1999, he has been held the chair of general modern history at the University of Zurich.

SEPP STRUBEL

Born in Worms (1939), grew up in Rheinhessen and the Palatine, messed up in a Swabian monastery school, trained in a Bavarian theatre school, Strubel landed in Augsburg – a south-German melange – in 1962. It is almost as though this city had a sort of "jus primae noctis" over me – first professional engagement at the Städtische Bühnen (city theatres) first speaking part at the Puppenkiste, first wife, first child, first professional theatre direction, first short films, first review as "particularly valuable", first screenplays, later first sculpture work, first exhibition, first large studio – naturally after so many early fixations the city just won't let me go. And always the old city, always the murmur and sounds of the canals, along the arteries. Now my first retirement – makes me restless. What does put me at ease: Life in the Lech district; hopefully for some time yet. On the Lech canals.

DR. CHRISTOF TREPESCH

Born in 1967 in Neunkirchen/Saar. Studied art history, classical archaeology, prehistory and early history at the University of Saarland. From 1993 to 2003 at the Saarlandmuseum Saarbrücken, most recently as acting chairman of the Saarland Cultural Holdings Foundation. Director of Kunstsammlungen und Museen Augsburg since 2004.

DR. RALF WITZLER

born a Rheinländer in 1964, studied in Bonn, received a doctorate in Greifswald. Internet editor of the Frankfurter Allgemeine Zeitung for several years; now head of the service at the financial news agency dpa-afx in the banking centre of Frankfurt. Author of several books and scientific publications on Brecht, Nietzsche and Foucault, and the foundation of technology-oriented companies. A passionate writer of travel reportage. A confessed friend of Augsburg for many years.

PHOTO CREDITS

Artothek, Peißenberg: S. 118
Augsburger Puppenkiste: S. 128/129 (3)
Bayerisches Hauptstaatsarchiv: Plan-Nr. 10718; S. 11
Bertolt-Brecht-Archiv, Berlin: S. 159
Blauel, Joachim: S. 117
Bleier, Christina: S. 114, 181 (3)
Brückelmair, Andreas: S. 24
Bunz, Achim: S. 112/113, 116
Eberlein, M., Archäologische Staatssammlung München: S. 27
Eisele, Helga Dr.: S. 16, 107, 143
Eisele, Reinhard: Umschlag, S. 4, 5, 8, 16/17 (4), 41, 42/43 (2), 44,
    45, 46, 47, 48, 49, 50, 51 (2), 53 (4), 56/57, 58 (3), 61 (2), 62 (2),
    64/65 (2), 66 (7), 68/69 (2), 70/71 (4), 72/73 (4), 74 (2), 75, 76/77,
    78 (2), 79 (2), 81 (3), 82 (3), 86, 87, 89 (4), 90 (5), 93 (6), 94, 97,
    100/101, 105, 109, 112, 132/133, 134, 136/137 (6), 139, 140,
    142/143 (5), 144 (2), 148, 149, 150, 151, 164, 165, 166/167 (2),
    170/171, 172, 173, 174, 175, 176/177, 178, 179, 182/183, 184, 186,
    187, 189
Fotomuseum im Münchner Stadtmuseum: S. 158 (2), 159 (3)
Fürstlich und gräflich Fuggersches Familien- und Stiftungsarchiv:
    S. 40
Herr, Elmar: S. 130 (3), 131 (4)
Hollo, Harald: S. 150, 151, 152/153 (4)
Kunstsammlungen und Museen Augsburg: S. 12, 13, 28/29, 31,
    32, 33, 34, 37, 96 (2), 98 (2), 99, 100, 101, 102, 103, 115, 119
Landesamt für Vermessung und Geoinformation Bayern ©:
    Topographische Karte 1:100 000, Nr. 5193/07; S. 15
Mozartsammlung Augsburg: S. 120, 123, 124, 125 (2)
Regio Augsburg Tourismus GmbH: S. 126
Römisches Museum: S. 21 (3), 22/23 (3), 27 (5)
Schreiber, Helmut: S. 18 (2), 19, 20, 36, 39, 42, 54, 61, 62, 65,
    82, 84, 106, 107, 108, 110/111 (2), 115, 132, 162/163 (3), 164,
    168/169 (3), 180
Staatsbibliothek Augsburg: S. 122, 154, 155, 156, 157 (2), 160
Stettmayer, Friedrich: S. 146/147, 148/149 (2)
Universitätsbibliothek Augsburg, Kartensammlung: S. 14
Wagner, Ulrich: S. 188
Wall, Anne: S. 120/121

PHOTO CREDITS, ACKNOWLEDGEMENT

©Andy Warhol Foundation for the Visual Arts/ARS, New York, 2007
    Warhol, Andy, S. 172
©Andy Warhol Foundation for the Visual Arts/ARS, New York, 2007
    Warhol, Andy, S. 173
©Dedalus Foundation, Inc./VG Bild-Kunst, Bonn 2007,
    Motherwell, Robert, Je t'aime, S. 172
©Dedalus Foundation, Inc./VG Bild-Kunst, Bonn 2007,
    Motherwell, Robert, Je t'aime, S. 173
©VG Bild-Kunst, Bonn 2007,
    Moris, Robert, Werk, S. 173
©VG Bild-Kunst, Bonn 2007,
    Geiger, Rupprecht, Pink contra Orange, S. 175

FOR THEIR INFORMATION AND HELP, WE THANK

Andreas Brücklmair
Manfred Hahn
Brigitte Herpich M. A.
Elmar Herr
Simone Kimmel M. A.
Dr. Peter Klimm
Christofer Kochs
Klaus Marschall
Loredana Melissari
Dr. Christoph Nicht
Bettina Seibert
Stephen Wood